Where We Are
American Catholics
in
The 1980s

Philip Scharper

Where We Are
American Catholics
in
The 1980s

꧁ ❋ ꧂

A Celebration for Philip Scharper

Edited by

Michael Glazier

 Michael Glazier, Inc.
Wilmington, Delaware

First published in 1985 by Michael Glazier, Inc, 1935 West Fourth Street, Wilmington, Delaware 19805. ©1985 by Michael Glazier, Inc. • Library of Congress Card Catalog Number: 85-45549 • International Standard Book Number: 0-89453-471-8 • Printed in the United States of America.

Contents

Introduction

We remember the gentle man who exuded courtesy, whose wry laughter and quiet scholarly ways blended with a delicate sensitivity; and we sensed that he was different. He was Philip Scharper. Christian and scholar and wonderful weaver of words, he clothed his spoken and written ideas with grace and dignity, and one sensed that here was a man moving to the music of creation.

Some lines from Maurice Baring's *Vale* come to mind:

I have loved words which lift the soul with wings,
Words that are windows to eternal things.
I have loved souls that to themselves are true,

Who cannot stoop and know not how to fear,
Yet hold the talisman of pity's tear:
I have loved these because I have loved you.

He stood apart from cliques and crusades; and was ever uneasy with the pundits, be they theologians or economists, who had lost the gift of listening to the strains of sadness and sorrow which shroud most human quests and questions. Gifted and haunted with a sense of mystery, he eschewed simple solutions and final answers to the problems or dilemmas that beset humankind. His was a pilgrim soul, ill at ease with the status quo, ever distrustful of teachers and leaders, clerical or lay, who acted as if they had the answers to every and any human problem.

There was about Philip an aura of cultured propriety, here was a man for whom courtesy was a very Christian thing. He did so many things gracefully and well, but we remember him especially as the bearer of gifts, verbal and otherwise, to all who crossed his way. He was the epitome of the Christian gentleman, the thoughtful christocentric man.

Many months before he passed to the new life on May 5, 1985, this book was in the making. A gift for Philip, a celebration and a *Deo gratias* for a sensitive and compassionate friend who touched and graced the lives of so many in expected and unexpected ways. In these pages, the few speak for the many who were enriched by knowing him, reading him, hearing him.

He would not care to be described as a man ahead of his times; rather, he was very attuned and sensitive to the moods and needs of these days. He was a man of vision who, though often surprised, was rarely impatient with the lack of foresight and insight in others. Philip was a bridgemaker for whom ecumenism was a human as well as a religious necessity. He stood in wonder with poets and prophets, convinced that caution was not a Christian way, confident that only the gamblers for God were fit to inherit the earth and the heavens.

Gazing on unscaled heights and new horizons, he enthused with those who said old denominational fences and borders corralled the human spirit. And as an editor he sought out writers who shared his view that theology was not history, that it was a vital and transforming experience rather than a venerated intellectual structure from another distant century.

When, over two decades ago, he become editor at Sheed & Ward, the very English and limited scope of its list was subtlely changed. He brought us the theological pacesetters of a new era: Rahner, Schillebeeckx, Küng. . . and their intellectual freshness whetted his hope of getting American Catholics thinking, writing and contributing to the fermenting theological dialogs of our times.

The primacy of conscience and religious freedom were precious in his sight, basic human rights—not commodities to be tolerated and dispensed at the convenience of church or state. He appreciated the importance and pertinence of the work and insights of John Courtney Murray, and he labored to clarify and shape the convoluted prose and nuanced thought of that American Jesuit genius, and readers got *We Hold These Truths*—and after Vatican II the Catholic church held them also.

Over a dozen years ago, he and Father Miguel d'Escoto, presently foreign minister of Nicaragua, launched Orbis Books, a forum for the theologies and cries of the dispossessed and the impoverished of the third, terrible world. Wise men shook their heads and the prudent prophesied publishing disaster. The odds were with the doubters. For years Alfred A. Knopf had unsuccessfully published the best of South American literature and reviewers and readers treated it with less than benign neglect. But Philip looked over the shoulders of difficulties and saw the Spirit

moving on the plains of our times. In a brief span of years
liberation theology altered the theological landscape of
America, showing us that a theology of the earthen bed
and the breadless table was far more important than most
of the theological musing in the halls of some seminaries
and colleges.

It was tempting to honor Philip with a book on the
various shades of liberation theology; but he, the most
American of men, would have been more curious about
the present outlook of American Catholics, whose attitudes have been questioned and somewhat broadened by
the vision of Gutierrez, Sobrino, Boff..., the spokesmen
of the impoverished whom Philip introduced to American
readers. Some of the contributors to this volume are well
known; all deserve to be more widely known. All are
doers of the Word and sharers in the dreams that made
Philip Scharper a person apart.

This book is for all the Scharper family. Philip and Sally
were inseparable: they were ever together, constant com-
panions, lovers of the language and of laughter; enthusi-
asts in ecumenism; constant in their commitment to
human and civil rights and ceaseless in their passionate
devotion to the needs of God's poor. And of their abun-
dance they gave to Sarah Katherine, Anne, Alice, David,
Philip and Stephen a caring and sharing home, where the
gospel meant more than grace before meals.

The Feast of All Saints, 1985.   *Michael Glazier*

American Catholicism Now

A Protestant View

Robert McAfee Brown

I am not going to give Philip Scharper all the credit for
whatever good things happen to American Catholicism in
the 1980's, but I am willing to consign a significant portion
of credit to him and to the ecclesiastical tugboat named
Orbis that he built and launched and captained (along with
some others) in order to nudge the barque of Peter into the
strong currents of contemporary life. Even an outsider
can observe that many on the larger vessel desire to return
to the eddys by the side of the stream, which seem safer
than the swifter currents elsewhere that threaten to
propel the vessel into uncharted waters. But Philip mus-
tered an able group of deckhands—with initially strange
names like Gutierrez, Boff, Boesak, Claver, Balasuriya,
Miranda and others—who had lived in the midst of those
swifter currents for a long time and could be counted on
not to bring the huge vessel to disaster, but to help it
function more creatively and less cumbersomely. To be

11

sure the captain of the larger vessel seems increasingly disenchanted with the nudging of the tugboat (particularly since it is also under his command), and is doing his best, along with a large curial crew, to resist the new directions.

It is anybody's guess who will win, and I'm willing to offer mine: given enough exposure to the new directions, those on the captain's bridge of the barque of Peter will ultimately discern that the direction in which the tugboat is nudging them is indeed the way they should go, and will yield to its suasive pressure. I only hope that in the interval between now and then, not too many inhabitants of either vessel will be accused of the last thing they have had in mind: plotting a mutiny.

The image had better be dropped before it gets completely out of hand, but it does at least signal the underlying viewpoint of the pages that follow.

The Past We All Inherited

One of my first ecumenical assignments came from Philip Scharper, then an editor at Sheed and Ward, who proposed a symposium in which Protestants and Jews would offer frank appraisals of American Catholicism. Such a project was almost unheard of at the time of its inception in 1957 or 1958, before Pope John or Vatican II had made their impact. Six of us contributed, four Protestants and two Jews, and Fr. Gustave Weigel, S.J., provided a Catholic afterword. *American Catholics: A Protestant-Jewish View*, Scharper, ed., (Sheed and Ward, New York, 1959, 235 pp.) did indeed initiate a kind of dialogue in the United States that had not taken place before. It was all Philip Scharper's doing.

In the light of my present assignment, to comment on American Catholicism in the 1980's, it may be instructive to review briefly where American Catholicism appeared to me to be in the late 1950's. At that time, the gap between Protestants and Catholics seemed totally insurmountable even as a conversation item, and I acknowledged at the outset that the dogma of papal infallibility was the stumbling block that made serious engagement between adherents of the two faiths seem remote. There were, nevertheless, "Areas of Catholic Creativity" even then that Protestants could observe: the liturgical movement, the "worker priest" movement, and the growing Catholic intellectual and theological ferment represented by such people as Yves Congar and Henri de Lubac. But *Humani Generis* had seemed to rebuke the latter, so the gains were fragile.

Easier to document were "Protestant Fears and Concerns About Catholicism," which were many, focusing either on the inner nature of Roman Catholicism (its apparent total control over the lives and thoughts of its constituents), and the relation of Catholicism to the rest of culture (its teaching on such issues as birth control, divorce, censorship, clericalism, public funds for parochial schools, legalizing bingo, and so forth). We Protestants really doubted at that time that Catholics, with their rigid hierarchical structure, could give more than expedient and temporary lip service to political democracy. The latter concern was usually spelled out by means of the "What if . . . ?" argument, implying, for example, that if Roman Catholics gained political control, the United States would become "another Spain," the Inquisition might be reintroduced, and so on. Our perception of the monolithic structure of the church fed such fears, and

queasiness about the degree of genuine Catholic acceptance of religious liberty made us fearful that Catholicism
in power would "impose" its ethic on the rest of us. Such
was our understanding of the Catholic view of authority
that it seemed as though there could never again be
significant reform of the church: "papalism" and the
dogmatic definition of infallible truths made that
impossible.

To most Protestants today and to many "liberal"
Catholics, such a laundry list of complaints may seem
quaint and amusing, so dated do many of them seem. Right
wing Catholics, however, may yearn nostalgically for a
day—not recoverable—when those indeed were the issues,
since they signalled the presence of a strong and unambiguous claim by the Catholic church to be the true flock of
the one true Shepherd.

A Past with Portents for the Future

What has happened in the meantime? A number of
things:

1. *The election of John F. Kennedy* in 1959, and his de-
meanor during his short presidency, put to rest most of the
fears about how "a Catholic in the White House" would
conduct himself. No hot lines to the Vatican were
installed, the public school system was not replaced by the
parochial school system, and non-Catholics continued to
be appointed to high positions of responsibility in the
government. An active anti-Catholic industry within
Protestantism collapsed for lack of targets to assault.

2. *The civil rights movement* of the early 1960's provided an
occasion when socially-minded Protestants and Catholics

found themselves side by side on marches, in picket lines, at the barricades, and in jail, and they formed deep friendships in common pursuit of goals that grew out of the shared aspects of their faith. They were increasingly unwilling to be isolated from one another in crisis situations, and those who found themselves sharing food at a prison table wondered with increasing intensity why they could not share food at the Lord's Table.

3. The impact of *"good Pope John"* and the Council he called into being challenged the received wisdom about such matters as papacy and irreformability. Here was a pope who fit no Protestant stereotypes, who was indeed "the good shepherd," wearing his badge of authority with charity rather than exclusivity, and here was a Council in which reform was not only *raison d'etre*, but the context of the discussion and the substance of the documents it produced.

4. The increasing emergence of *lay Catholic voices*, the creation of such instruments as the *National Catholic Reporter* and the ongoing influence of *Commonweal* (for which Philip had also worked), dispelled the "priest-ridden" image of the church that many Protestants had, and demonstrated that internal critique from below was indeed a possibility in the Catholic church. The Vietnam war, which aroused little Roman Catholic episcopal critique until near the end, also helped to develop lay voices and acts, and brought about the escalation of Catholic lay protest through the emergence of the "Catholic left"—a term Protestants would previously have felt to be self-cancelling. Members of this constituency soon outstripped their Protestant counterparts, as priests and sisters in addition to lay people took increasingly public roles in protest and civil disobedience.

5. A further contributing factor to U.S. Catholic maturity was *the domestic impact of new movement in Catholicism elsewhere*, most notably the emergence of liberation theology in Latin America in the early 1970's and its implicit blessing in advance at the conference of Latin American bishops at Medellin in 1968. As information about new currents of political involvement by Catholics in Latin America filtered up to North America, the face of North American Catholicism began to change, not only in terms of confronting new dimensions of the faith that third world voices articulated, but also in forcing new realization of the complicity of North Americans in the structures of injustice that were contributing factors to poverty in Latin America.

Notable in the Medellin documents were such things as a new method of social analysis, taking "systemic evil" seriously and not confining sin to the private arena of the individual heart, a new stress on justice as the lodestone for ecclesiastical direction, and a view of the church that (rather unexpectedly) led to the almost spontaneous emergence of tens of thousands of *comunidades de base*, "base communities" or grassroots communities of Catholics, gathered in groups of 15 or 20 for Bible study, prayer and reflection on social evils that needed to be combatted in the name of the gospel. These represent the genuine fruit of Medellin, reaching across the church, and breaking through class and hierarchical lines in marvelous ways.

6. The chief reason why North Americans began to learn about liberation theology and the new movements of spiritual maturity that spun off from it in Latin America, was the coming into being of *Orbis Books*. In June 1970 the Maryknoll religious order sparked by the guidance of Philip Scharper, launched this publishing project "to

make Americans more aware of and responsive to the problems of the third world, those emerging nations of Asia, Africa and Latin America, where two-thirds of the world's people live."

This was a risky venture—who in North America would want to read theology originating in Asia, Africa or Latin America? A few perhaps, but surely not enough to enable such a venture to succeed... Such pessimism was unfounded. Orbis not only reached the few, but created a market that shifted the whole tone and locus of theological discussion. Once the writings of the Latin Americans (and later the Africans and Asians) began to be translated and published in the United States, they not only introduced new emphases and interpretations of the Christian faith, but had to be accepted as contributing partners to the global theological discussion that had heretoforth ignored them.

In 1978, writing for *The Ecumenist*, I commented, "I would venture the guess that in the last eight years Orbis Books, more than any other single agency on the North American scene, has helped contemporary Christians to look at the world in new ways." Not only would I stand by that statement seven years further down the line, but I would remove the hesitant qualifier "I would venture the guess..." The influence of Orbis not only on the Catholic scene, but the entire religious and secular scene, is beyond dispute. Indeed, the fact that such right wing Catholics as William F. Buckley, Jr., Andrew Greeley and Michael Novak are unremitting in their attacks on Orbis Books is a back-handed tribute to the influence Orbis has come to have on the literary and ecclesiastical scene. One does not waste time attacking that which is inconsequential. With such enemies, who needs friends?

Looking to the Recent Past

As we look briefly at the first half of the 1980's, we can see further signs of openings in American Catholicism.

1. Let us situate *the Puebla conference* of the Latin American bishops, held in 1979, within the present rubric, since its impact has been a phenomenon of the 1980's and has clearly extended north of the Rio Grande. It is well-known that conservatives within the church, from Archbishop Lopez Trujillo on down (or up) had hoped at Puebla to mute the voice of liberation theology and clip the wings of the *comunidades de base*. The quick and accurate response is that both attempts failed. Liberation theology and the base communities emerged stronger than before in the Puebla texts, which also made normative for contemporary Catholic thought a commitment by the church to make a "preferential option for the poor." (The succeeding section of the Puebla document also called for a "preferential option for youth," a theme that has been virtually forgotten in the subsequent discussion.)

2. An important event in American Catholic life was the issuing of the final draft of *the bishops' letter on nuclear weapons*. The product of an extraordinary amount of listening and discussing and grass roots consulting, this document took strong initiatives in articulating the fears and the hopes of millions of Americans facing a nuclear age without much sense of direction. The bishops' letter does not pretend to be a final word, but it remains a significant catalyst for other words and commitments to action, far beyond the confines of the Catholic church. As a Protestant, I have found it the single most useful document on the subject, both in my teaching and in working with church groups. There is cause for amazement, as well as evidence

of the reality of the Holy Spirit, that the American bishops, so tardy in their acknowledgement of the evils of the Vietnam war, should within a decade have emerged as the moral leaders of the nation in challenging conventional wisdom surrounding nuclear weapons.

3. This emergence on the political scene has not been productive of serenity between *church and state*. Particularly around the 1984 presidential election, the issue of "religion and politics" re-emerged full blown. Part of this was precipitated by the right wing of Protestantism, the fundamentalist groups such as Moral Majority. Having belatedly discovered that religion and politics do mix after all, they began to make amends for lost time by espousing the Reagan cause unabashedly, giving a religious justification for prayer in public schools, anti-abortion legislation, attacks on "secular humanism" and communism (which were frequently equated), and the like. Nor were Catholics reticent to enter the arena, and much heat, if little light, was engendered by debates over whether Catholics could in good conscience vote for candidates who in good conscience were pro-choice on the abortion issue. When New York's archbishop John O'Connor's implicit "no" on this matter gave a pretty clear message that Catholics could not vote for Geraldine Ferraro, this left a slate for Catholics on which only the names of Ronald Reagan and George Bush remained, Bush having conveniently recanted his former pro-choice position just in time.

The issues will remain—both the morality or immorality of abortion, and the appropriateness or inappropriateness of episcopal fiats in the political realm.

4. We must also take note of *conservative movements*. Such matters as the bishops' letter on nuclear weapons provoked strong right wing protests both inside and outside

the church, and while papal journeys across the globe sometimes produced forthright statements on social justice, they more frequently stressed such themes as obedience to the hierarchy, and explicitly ruled out any thought of modification on such issues as women priests, married clergy, birth control, abortions, greater autonomy for religious orders, and so on. Forces in Rome were rallied against liberation theology, and a letter from the Sacred Congregation of the Doctrine of the Faith took strong issue with liberation theology at two points: (1) the presumed dependence of liberation theology on Marxist categories of interpretation, a charge aimed particularly at Gustavo Gutierrez, and (2) the presumed challenge to the authority of the hierarchical church by the base communities, a charge aimed particularly at Leonardo Boff. Both individuals were in Rome in September 1984 to give an accounting of themselves, and although there were no condemnations at that time, it was clear that the matter was far from closed.

Other issues beginning to surface in the first half of the 1980's can be better appraised by turning our glance ahead.

Looking to the Future

What will be the "shape" of American Catholicism in the last half of the 1980's?

1. I anticipate that the authorities in Rome will make increasing attempts to stifle, if not scuttle, *liberation theology*. The "silencing" of Leonardo Boff (announced as these pages were being written) is the latest ominous portent. My own conviction, as an outsider, is that this

tactic will not work. The "cry of the people" for justice is not going to be silenced, and the way that cry is expressed from below will not be controllable from on high. The fact that liberation theology is so patently biblical, and draws so fully on Catholic tradition (as evidenced in Gutierrez' recent *We Drink From Our Own Wells*) is the ultimate assurance not only of its survival but also of its growth.

2. Continued discussion will center on successive drafts of *the bishops' letter on the economy*. This document, which even in its initial draft seems to me a notable theological and ecclesiological contribution, is bound to shape much of the subsequent discussion in Protestant as well as Catholic circles, and, let us hope, in so-called "secular" circles as well. The ill-timed "layman's letter" (a "response" to the bishops' letter that was published even before the object of its attack had been released) certainly generates little response in Protestant circles, although we can expect its adherents to continue to try to modify the bishops' stands, stands that nevertheless seem likely to survive handily. There is a curious reversal here: in the 1950's, it seemed as though the hope of Roman Catholicism was located in lay voices challenging the social somnolence of the hierarchy; now, thirty years later, it is the hierarchy that has taken over leadership on social issues, with right wing laity sounding alarms about the presumed "radicalism" of the bishops.

3. There is to be a bishops' letter on *the role and status of women in the church*. I wish the bishops all the best on this one, while simultaneously fearing that even my genial good wishes will not suffice to get such a document off the ground in a fashion comparable to the letters on nuclear weapons or the economy. For the American bishops face

an ecclesiastical Catch 22 situation: no breakthrough on the role of women in the church can come without approval from Rome, and approval from Rome of breakthrough on the role of women in the church is not going to come—at least not in our life-times. As a non-Catholic who is firmly committed to rights of women to a full life within Christ's church, including ordination, I am personally sad to have to record this prognosis, but I realize that the Protestant contribution to the role of women in the church will not come by carping from the outside, but by giving as clear and unambiguous a witness as possible within our own communions to the viability, desirability and necessity of full citizenship within the church.

Short of the canonical approval of women's ordination which will not be forthcoming, I nevertheless see two important ways in which the role of women can continue to be strengthened in the near future. One of these is represented by the increasing seizing of initiative by women religious. I know that this is a source of consternation in Rome—as well it might be if Rome's real goal is to make women once more subordinate to the process of male hierarchical decision-making. My own theological announcement is that the Holy Spirit has other plans, and that in the decades ahead the Catholic sisters are going to be the secret (and sometimes not so secret) arm of that same Spirit. Nothing in contemporary American Catholic life impresses me more than the vitality, the courage, and the integrity of women religious, and I see their role to be one of increasing significance in the lives of all of us, whether Catholic or not, whatever may be the temporary setbacks they endure in the present dispensation.

There are probably many reasons for feminist initiatives within Roman Catholicism of which I am necessarily unaware, but I believe that in the church at large part of the prophetic upsurge is due to a rediscovery, or at least a redefinition, of the role of Mary. Mary, once almost anathema to Protestants, is now emerging as an important rallying point in social justice struggles—the Mary of the Magnificat rather than the Mary of the holy pictures, and it is my perception that this is happening in Catholicism as well. Rather than the demure passive maiden dressed in blue, we now have the powerful leader whose home is with the oppressed of the world, and who enlists our support to see that the hungry are fed and the poor are lifted up.

4. Offsetting some of this will be the ongoing voice of the *conservative wing* of American Catholicism, already noted above, genuinely fearful that Vatican II will continue to be employed by others to unravel the threads of the seamless robe of Christ. It is not for an outsider to judge what must endure—before, during and after Vatican II—in the theological arena of Catholicism, but what distresses one is the way in which an emerging right wing theology is wedded to right wing politics and economics in such a way that the latter emerges as the real bottom line. When, for example, members of this faction want to buttress their dissatisfaction with the left-wing regime in Nicaragua, they cite the Nicaraguan bishops against the laity, and when they want to buttress their dissatisfaction with presumed left-wing tendencies in the United States, they cite the American laity against the bishops. The authority acceded to the bishops seems to depend on where they stand on an economic, rather than a theological, spectrum.

5. The *role of the pope* remains an unresolved enigma to me, though I find a lot of my Catholic friends are sharing

this dilemma. On some social justice issues, the pope has exerted creative leadership; no one who says, "There is a social mortgage on all private property" can be confined in a reactionary box. At the same time, I feel the pain of many sensitive Catholics on the papal intransigence exhibited in areas previously referred to where they want at least some discussion on matters of internal reform: ordination of women and married men, birth control, greater freedom for women religious, the legitimacy of liberation theology, and so on. It is sad to observe people of immense good will and utter integrity forced continually to reappraise their relationship to institutional Catholicism for reasons of conscience.

6. A final prediction: movements like *Orbis Books* will flourish. As we have noted, there have been a number of attempts to undermine the edifice of Orbis over the last few years, and happily they have failed. I believe there will be increasing numbers of Catholics and Protestants who will employ the Orbis book list as a bibliographical guide to the really important theological reading through the rest of the century. Along with many others, we will stand indebted to the original vision of Philip Scharper, Miguel d'Escoto, John Eagleson and the Maryknoll order who were willing to launch the project.

The influence of Philip as a bridge-builder across languages, cultures and nationalities was beautifully illustrated to me during a trip to Nicaragua during Holy Week of 1985, about two months after Philip's stroke and shortly before his death. I was there with an ecumenical fact-finding team, and our last appointment was with Fr. Miguel d'Escoto, a Maryknoll priest, co-founder with Philip of Orbis Books, and also—as the world knows—Minister of Foreign Affairs for the Sandinista government. He was just back from several days in Brazil, dead tired, inundated with back work, and immediately facing the necessity of trying to make the Nicaraguan "case" to a group of people from a country that is systematically trying to destroy his country. He was surrounded, in other words, with the most harassing and demanding affairs of state. But when we came into the room and I spoke to him, his immediate response was not, "Let me explain our attitude about the *contras*," or "Please tell me why your govenment is trying to deny us agricultural assistance," but simply, "I am so distressed about our friend Phil."

Looking South from Canada

❧✻❧

Gregory Baum

Looking south to the Unites States, to the country that owns most of our industries, I am guided by the social and economic analysis provided by Pope John Paul II and the Canadian Catholic bishops.[1] These churchmen have argued that the world capitalist system is entering a new phase at this time, one characterized by great brutality. In an earlier phase, in the U.S. beginning with the New Deal, capitalism committed itself to the society in which it operated. Since the capitalists realized that they needed the cooperation of society, they were willing to enter into an unwritten contract with it, guaranteeing full employment, welfare measures, and respect for labor organiza-

[1]For the main social messages of the Canadian Catholic bishops and a commentary on their controversial "Ethical Reflections on the Economic Crisis," see, G. Baum and D. Cameron, *Ethics and Economics*, (Toronto: Lorimer, 1984); Cf., G. Baum, "Beginnings of a Canadian Catholic Social Theory," in S. Brooks, ed., *Political Thought in Canada*, (Toronto: Irwin, 1984), pp. 49-80.

tions. There are many signs that this phase of capitalism has come to an end. The unwritten contract is being dissolved. Because of several historical developments, capitalism is reorganizing itself on an international scale around the giant corporations that control a large part of the world economy. Capitalist production no longer needs the whole of society to support it. International mobility allows corporations to engage in production wherever the conditions are most advantageous for them; and high technology delivers them from dependency upon masses of workers. The new orientation of capitalism leads to the exclusion of growing sectors of the population from work and from wages. This is true for Canada. And this is also true, even if on a slightly smaller scale, for the United States.

Because of the presence of transnational corporations in the Third World, these countries are unable to organize their own self-reliant economic development, based on their resources, their skills and talents, and on markets among their own people. According to the Canadian bishops, the economic system that widens the gap between rich and poor in Canada also widens the gap between rich and poor countries in the world. On his visit to Canada, Pope John Paul II had this to say about the widening gap between North and South: "Poor people and poor nations — poor in different ways, not only lacking food, but also deprived of freedom and other human rights — will sit in judgement on those people who take these goods away from them, amassing to themselves the imperialistic monopoly of economic and political supremacy at the expense of others" (Edmonton, 17 Sept. 1984). This is how the Catholic Church is teaching me to look south of the border.

The American quest for economic and political su-

premacy is closely related to the nuclear arms race that
threatens humanity at this time. The two Superpowers
stand over against one another. At the same time, the
East-West conflict and the Cold War climate also have
their convenience for the two Superpowers. It allows the
U.S. government to interpret the conflicts in Third
World countries and its own active role in their politics in
terms of the competing interests of East and West. In their
pastoral on the U.S. economy, the American Catholic
bishops themselves complain that the U.S. government
reads North-South problems in East-West terms and
regards the conflicts in Third World countries as test cases
in the East-West struggle.[2] The poor countries, the American bishops lament, have meaning and value for the U.S.
government only in terms of a larger geo-political calcu-
lus. The Cold War and the nuclear build-up have their
usefulness: they justify, in the name of national security,
the harsh policies of political intervention and social control intended to pacify and keep powerless the growing
sector of the world population excluded from bread, from
work, and from participation.

In a joint statement on nuclear weapons, the Canadian
Churches drew this conclusion: "Nuclear weapons are
becoming part of the means by which Northern industrial
states compete for influence and domination in the Third
World and by which they seek to keep in place a world
economic order that bestows extraordinary costs on the
powerless."[3] Again, this is how the Churches teach me to

[2]"First Draft—Bishop's Pastoral: Catholic Social Teaching and the U.S.
Economy," *Origins: NC documentary service* 14 (15 November 1984) no. 290, p.
372.

[3]Statement of Dec. 8, 1982, signed by representatives of the Anglican
Church, the Catholic Church, the Lutheran Church, the Presbyterian Church
and the United Church of Canada, *The Ecumenist* 21 (Sept.-Oct. 1983) 91.

look south. For the most part, let me add, the present Canadian government supports, with minor reservations, the policies of the United States.

What are the human costs of these structural changes in the economy? In recent years the Christian Churches have produced many documents that describe and analyze the human misery produced by the expanding structures of exclusion, due to unemployment, poverty, and various forms of discrimination inflicted on non-whites, on women, and on young people. These human costs have become so high that the Canadian bishops have called present unemployment a sinful condition.

What are the cultural consequences of this structural shift in the economy? We are witnessing in the U.S.A. and Canada (and possibly in the whole of Western industrial society) the creation of a culture, sometimes called "neo-conservative," that tries to reconcile people with the unequal distribution of wealth and power: this culture evaluates the protest movements of the Sixties as utopian and childish, generates anti-socialist sentiment and honors the self-made man, makes individualism and indifference to the suffering of others respectable, and rejoices in United States power as the guardian of freedom and prosperity. As the circle of wealth and security is continually shrinking, people hope and tremble that they, at least, will not be pushed into the margin but be allowed to stay among the comfortable. Thus they are ready to defend the existing order, dispense themselves from social solidarity, and make great efforts to climb to a safer place within the system. We are witnessing the return of a class society with clearly marked boundaries. Since attendence at universities is becoming increasingly expensive, the students easily see themselves as belonging to a class destined for success: they often become indifferent to social justice and seek a philosophy that justifies their unabashed self-interest. During the last election campaign in the U.S., even the Democratic Party in opposition refused to offer an alternative vision of American society. To gain electoral support from the American people, the Party decided not to deviate too much from the present economic, political and cultural orientation.

There are of course minority movements in the U.S.A. and the Western world which go against the stream. Among them stand out, for all to see, the Christian Churches. People are not used to seeing the Church so clearly on the progressive side. Canadian Catholics who are proud of their own bishops also look with admiration to the bishops of the United States who, in two important pastoral letters, applied an evangelical test to the orientation of American society and then opposed the nuclear, economic and political policies of the government. Learning from the Church in Latin America and the teaching of John Paul II, and relying on the message emerging from the growing network of Christian groups committed to justice in North America, the bishops of Canada and the United States have made the preferential option for the poor. They are willing to look upon their society and the world as a whole from the perspective of the poor and marginalized.

Canadians find in the pastoral letter on the U.S. economy a language somewhat different from their own.[4] The American bishops recall the revolutionary origin of the Republic. The first American experiment was the creation of democratic institutions to protect the political rights of citizens. Since that time America has become the

[4]For a comparison between the social teaching of the U.S. and the Canadian bishops, see G. Baum, *Christianity and Crisis* (January 21, 1985).

wealthiest and most powerful nation in the world, on whose political and economic policies the well-being of a wide sector of humanity depends. The time has come, the U.S. bishops argue, seeing the great suffering of the marginalized in the U.S. and in the world, for "a new American experiment" to extend democracy to the economic sphere, demand public accountability of the giant corporations and complete the inherited civil liberties with people's economic rights, i.e., the rights to participate in the production and distribution of wealth. The bishops call the American people to a new cultural and spiritual perception of themselves; they denounce the widespread individualism and selfishness and summon people to social solidarity as the realistic context for personal development and personal happiness.

Canadian Catholics who agree with the social teaching of their own bishops look south to the Catholic Church in the U.S. with great admiration. They realize of course that just as only a minority of Canadian Catholics follow their bishops' bold social teaching, so only a minority of Catholics in the U.S.A. adopt the perspective of their bishops and endorse the preferential option for the poor. Still, in our countries, the Church has become prophet. I regard this ecclesiastical evolution as an event of world historical importance. What Church welcomed by empire has ever stood up against it? What Church welcomed by the state has ever condemned the preparation for war? What Church woven into an existing economic system has ever become a prophetic critic of it, risking its own financial base? It is true that compared with the critique of capitalism offered by the Canadian bishops, the social message of the American bishops is more accommodating; still, speaking from inside the Superpower, the American bishops clearly stand against empire and domi-

nation, demand justice in America, and make justice the
norm that must regulate the relation of America to the
world economy. In the past, the Christian groups we
called "the sects" have sometimes been capable of such
witness; the Churches on the whole were not. The stance
the Catholic Church, seconded by the other Christian
Churches, has taken in the American Empire is part of a
series of events that signal a profound reorientation of
Christianity in the contemporary world.

These historical events are grounded in new Christian
experiences. A new spiritual orientation is emerging.
What is taking place in the Church, Johann Baptist Metz
has suggested, is the recovery of the Synoptic Jesus. We
are regaining access to Jesus preaching his own message,
Jesus pronouncing the beatitudes, Jesus proclaiming God's
approaching reign, Jesus in search of disciples, Jesus pronouncing his woes upon his opponent and not shrinking
from making enemies, Jesus persecuted, slandered,
mocked and humiliated, imprisoned, condemned by a
court and eventually executed. Blessed are the poor: God
is with them, God stirs them up, they are bearers of the
divine promise. Blessed are those who mourn: they are
unable to disassociate themselves from the suffering of
others, they experience solidarity with the poor, God is
present among them too. Blessed are the meek: they do
not try to escape the condition of oppression individually,
they remain in solidarity with their brothers and sisters.
Blessed are the peace-makers: they oppose nuclear weapons, and in doing so they discover the impulses toward
war in their own society. God is present to them in their
resistance to violence. Blessed are those who hunger and
thirst after justice: God is alive in the hearts of those who
yearn and struggle for a more human world. Blessed are
those who experience persecution for the sake of God's

reign: those who oppose the power of domination are vulnerable, they have the police sent after them, in some countries they suffer imprisonment, torture and death, the God of the poor embraces these victims. The God of the poor has the power to restore to life those whom a wicked society has pushed into death by hunger, military force, concentration camps, and war machines. Blessed are the merciful; they do not seek revenge for the oppression inflicted on them, revenge perpetuates violence, they yearn instead for a qualitatively new society in which all can be brothers and sisters. A certain middle-class-based scholarship tended to see in the preaching of the Synoptic Jesus an "interim ethics" applicable only in his day when Christians eagerly awaited the end of history; today many Christians are rediscovering the abiding relevance of the beatitudes and the call to discipleship.[5]

From the preceding I conclude that the Catholic Church in the U.S.A. has moved to a new, prophetic stance in regard to the nation and the world. I regard this as an enormously important event, the full significance of which emerges only in connection with similar changes taking place in other parts of the world. There is, however, another important role which, I think, the American Catholic Church should and will play within Roman Catholicism as a whole. Allow me to develop this second point.

A growing number of Catholics, including Catholic bishops, have become convinced that the norms for a just society, spelled out in Catholic social teaching, also apply to the Church itself. In their pastoral on the U.S. economy the American bishops define injustice in terms of margin-

[5]Cf., Homily on the meaning of the beatitudes today, given by Pope John Paul II during his Canadian visit at Ottawa, 20 September 1984, *The Canadian Catholic Review* 2 (Oct. 1984) 78-80.

alization, i.e., the structural exclusion of people from access to power and responsibility; and they define justice in terms of the overcoming of marginalization through participation.[6] If this ethical norm were aplied to the Catholic Church itself, one would be obliged to make a very negative judgement in regard to ecclesiastical institutions. The Catholic Church has inherited a tradition of monocratic power. We have inherited the prejudice that the order of a community can only be guaranteed if a single person, a man, is put in charge. Order is from the top down. The synodal and collegial traditions have been almost totally forgotten over the centuries. The Catholic Church saw itself committed to the principle of one-man-rule: the pope over the universal church, the bishop over his diocese, the pastor over the parish: wherever ecclesiastical superiors were appointed, they thought of their authority in a monocratic way. A few religious orders retained certain collegial practices derived from their original foundation.

The attempt of Vatican Council II to retrieve the collegial tradition has had a certain success, especially in creating national episcopal conferences with a sense of collective responsibility. According to Vatican II, the bishop is not only the head of his diocese, he is also especially coresponsible with other bishops for the regional church, the national church, and the worldwide church. Thanks to the principle of collegiality, the pope is not understood as exercising the highest authority alone: as head of the Church he is accompanied by the entire episcopate. In recent years, the national episcopal conferences have been fruitful manifestations of collegiality. In particular, the process adopted by the American bishops

[6]"First Draft," ibid., no. 90-94, p. 351.

in elaborating their major pastoral letters on nuclear weapons and the U.S. economy was an exercise in participation.

Justice demands participation. At the same time, the trend toward participation also finds its opposition in the Church. The Vatican itself sends many messages that seem to discourage participation. Outstanding is here the refusal of the Congregation for Religious to allow the religious congregations of women in America to introduce democratic elements into their constitutions. The Roman Congregation assumes that monocratic power is the only valid understanding of authority in the Church. Against this narrow ecclesiastical trend, the Latin American Bishops Conference at Puebla (1979) called for "the self-evangelization of the Church," that is to say the conversion to the Gospel of persons and institutions in Church.[7] One of the norms by which ecclesiastical institutions should be examined and reformed is "participation." The demand for greater participation presupposes that the guidance of the Church is the work of the Holy Spirit, and that this takes place through the conscience and fidelity of all the members. What is necessary, therefore, are structures of dialogue, consultation, and participation that will allow the divine guidance to come to the surface and influence the Church's pastoral policy at the top.

The opposition to participation by churchmen attached to the old monocratic style is no longer articulated in theoretical form. On a theological level, everyone realizes that the norms of justice spelled out by Catholic social teaching, also apply to the church. The 1971 Synod of Bishops insisted on this point. "While the Church is bound to give witness to justice, she recognizes that anyone who

[7]"Puebla Document," n. 228, see J. Eagleson, ed., *Puebla and Beyond*, (Maryknoll, N.Y.: Orbis Books, 1979) p. 152.

ventures to speak to people about justice must first be just
in their eyes. Hence we must undertake an examination of
the modes of acting and of the possessions and life style
found within the Church itself."[8] According to the 1971
Synod, "rights must be preserved in the Church." This
includes "the right of everyone to be heard in a spirit of
dialogue which preserves a legitimate diversity in the
Church."[9] At present these rights are not protected by any
institutions. There is no division between the legislative
and the judicial powers in the Church, a situation unique
in Western societies. There are no independent courts in
the Church to protect members from an irresponsible
exercise of authority. There are no legally recognized
forums in the Church where people judged by the authorities can explain and defend their point of view. Justice
demands that people have the right to have their voices
heard before important decisions are made that affect
their lives. At present there is no such legal requirement
for the appointments of bishops. This is unjust.

Over the last years, a growing number of authoritarian
decisions made at the Vatican and by some local ordinaries, in violation of the norms of justice, have caused great
scandal among Catholics whose ethical standards have
been formed by a democratic culture. In earlier periods of
history, Catholics were ready to accept a certain mystique
of obedience and credited the office bearer with a special
divine guidance that dispensed him from dialogue and
consultation. At one time this was the accepted way, not
out of step with the political culture of society and recognized ethical standards. Today this has changed. Democracy has created an ethical aspiration at odds with

[8]"*Justitia in mundo*," no. 40, see J. Gremillion, ed., *The Gospel of Peace and Justice*, (Maryknoll, N.Y.: Orbis Books, 1976) p. 522.
[9]Ibid., no. 44.

traditional ecclesiastical practice. More than that, the 20th century has experienced the danger of authoritarianism in the emergence of fascist and communist mystiques of obedience. Fascist and communist notions of authority and obedience aim at the enhancement of the collective good in disregard of the private good, which is the dignity of the individual. Persons here become instruments to promote the advancement of the collectivity. In the early Thirties some Catholics in Germany believed that there was a certain affinity between the fascist "Fuhrerprinzip" and the Catholic concept of authority and obedience.[10] Yet since that time, Catholics have come to insist that the only appropriate exercise of authority is one that honors the dignity of persons and hence has a certain dialogue structure. There is a qualitative difference between fascist and Catholic notions of authority. By its very nature, authority in the Church is open to participation. The common good demands that decisions be made by the competent authority, decisions that have to be followed, but in the process of arriving at these decisions the dignity of persons must be recognized and hence there should be conversation, consultation and electoral procedures. While authority in the Church is divinely grounded, authoritarianism is a distortion.

Because there is no longer any sound theological basis for the old style of monocratic authority in the Church, the opponents of participation, at the Vatican and in certain dioceses, now sometimes act in irrational and resentment-laden ways. They make arbitrary judgements, they condemn books without offering explanations, they dismiss seminary professors without due

---

[10]Cf., Klemens Richer, ed., *Die katholische Kirche und das Judentum*, (Freiburg: Herder, 1982) p. 104.

process, they remove people from pastoral programs without allowing them to defend themselves, they demand total control over their priests, and at the same time they dispense themselves from following the pastoral directives and social teaching of the Church as a whole. Authoritarianism lies like a curse on the Catholic tradition, a counter-sign to the Gospel, a sinful element from which the Catholic Church yearns to be delivered.

Since the Catholic Church in the U.S.A. shares in the democratic tradition derived from the American revolution, and since the American bishops over the last decade have expanded dialogue and consultation and created a new, participatory process for elaborating the two important pastorals on nuclear weapons and the U.S. economy, the American Catholic Church may well be the historical actor through which God will deliver the Catholic tradition from the curse of authoritarianism. The American Church, relying on the Christian elements in the best of the American cultural tradition, may be the only institutions in the wider Catholic Church that could convince church leaders, including the Vatican, that participation is not antithetical to authority, that dialogue is not at odds with obedience, and that principled criticism of church government is not disloyal but a necessary corrective for blindness at the top. The best religious way of educating young people to assume responsibility in society is to admit them to participation in their own parishes and churches.

Looking at the world today makes me fearful, but looking at the Church today, and especially at the Church in the U.S.A, gives me hope.

Urgencies of the '80s
Young People and Women

✺

John Deedy

Several years ago, when I was plying my trade in New York, I and two colleagues had lunch at the Williams Club with a prominent Catholic politician. He was no run-of-the pew Catholic politician. When he entered the dining room, heads turned, and why not? He had stood twice for the presidency. I won't mention his name, but you can guess. It was the time of great upheaval in American Catholicism, when priests were leaving, when nuns were leaving, when the churches were being emptied of worshippers. Everything seemed downhill. "How about you?," our guest was asked. "Are you still making it to Mass on Sunday?" Maybe it was an impertinent question, one's Sunday habits being one's own business. Besides, since when did regular Sunday mass attendance define orthodoxy? If our guest was disconcerted, he didn't show it. "Listen," he answered. "I've come this far. I'm not going to be shot down by a legalism."

I've thought about that exchange thousands of times since. The more I do the more I am struck how much the response measures the distance between the senior generations of American Catholics and so many more of the new generations.[1] Not that in both groups there are not sincere, conscientious, committed believers. I'm only saying that we older Catholics, who grew up in a faith where legalism counted for so much, find it hard to shake those legalisms, so that for very many of us, much of faith and the practice of religion are part impulse, part legalistic habit. There's nothing wrong with that, but we must realize that, when we drop a generation or so down the age scale, legalisms mean absolutely nothing. Those of the younger generations who are regular, practicing Catholics are active because they choose to be, not because some legalism hangs over their head. That's as it should be, but, alas, the numbers of such believers are thin, I am afraid.

Wait. I know what the surveys say about Catholic religious indifference bottoming out and about there being an up-turn in church attendance and accordingly in the formal practice of religion. Maybe it's because I live in a small cape town on the end of the land, a community not representative of urban America, but I just don't see it that way. I look around me in church and there's a huge age-gap. There are the greying and the balding on the one hand, and the pre-high schoolers on the other, with relatively few in between. There seem to be more dropout Catholics than you can shake a crozier at.

Nor do articles like Fran Schumer's "A Return to Religion" in the April 15, 1984 *New York Times Magazine*

[1]Considering ours, in an age of improved medicine and expanding longevity, to be a four-generation society, the dividing line between the senior and new or younger generations for purposed of this essay would be around 40.

persuade me that there is a significant, much less "tremendous" resurgence of religious interest. Harvard's Harvey Cox is invoked, as Ms. Schumer reports more students wearing crosses or yarmulkes on campuses. *Commonweal*'s Peter Steinfels is quoted as saying, "There is the sympathetic entertainment of religious belief in intellectual circles that you wouldn't have detected ten years ago." Ms. Schumer argues that "unlike the more impassioned swing to 'born-again' Christianity of recent years, and to Eastern Religions in the late 1960s, this revival is a more sober affair." Robert N. Bellah adds, "There is a reaction against extreme individualism and self, a preoccupation with and a search for roots with a capital R, which takes people back to religion. Tradition is back on the agenda with a positive force."

Well, I'm not exactly sure that is so on the institution's parish level, at least so far as the new generations are concerned. Good grief, even in my little town, the parish church cannot be open apart from the regular hours of worship out of fear of vandalism. There's nothing like a locked church to suggest to young people that religion is a sometime thing. In any instance, I don't see at the Catholic parish level what Ms. Schumer sees elsewhere in the land. When I do see young people in church, so often they seem restrained and tentative, almost as if they were strangers to the new liturgy. No doubt many are. I will never forget the look of utter surprise on the face of an early-middle-age women with two aged parents in tow at Christmas Mass a few years ago, when the moment came for the exchange of the sign of peace. The aged couple, familiar with what was going on, moved naturally with the rhythm of the liturgy. Not so the daughter. Quite obviously she was situated back when it was the priests on the altar who exchanged the sign of peace, not the people in the pews. There was great wonderment on her face, which changed to beaming grin. Whether her practice was affected by the occasion at hand, I have no notion. I saw the parents together at Mass many Sundays hence. The daughter may have been back in California or someplace.

Take another example. I've been to several weddings the past two years and an unhappy number of funerals, and what happens when communion-time arrives? Virtually everyone receives in the hand, the exceptions being a few hold-out older men and women, *and* many of the younger generation. Are the latter liturgical conservatives like the hold-out older folks? Is this an act of piety and devotion on their part? Or could it be that they've been so long absent from church that they are unfamiliar with the change in policy allowing communion in the hand? Could it be that the last time they were to communion one received one way — on the tongue?

Those may be very presumptuous questions, but they reflect the fact that there are millions of American Catholics who are Catholic in name only. Their situation should be an urgent item of business for the American Catholic Church for the 1980s. But it doesn't seem to be, though at one time it was supposed to be.

In 1978, the National Conference of Catholic Bishops at a spring meeting in Chicago estimated that there were 68 million Americans with no church affiliation and, more pertinently, that there were 12 million non-practicing American Catholics (a conservative estimate perhaps, but a whopping number nonetheless). The bishops accordingly announced plans for a major evangelical effort aimed at the unchurched. The details were not yet completed and the bishops said they wouldn't be until late 1979, but the effort was to be mounted and it would utilize mass media and the resources of the 18,000 Catholic parishes across the country. The program was to carry, as I recall, over five years' time. Has anyone heard of the problem or the program since its announcement? I haven't. Since 1971 I have been writing the Roman Catholic Church entry in the *Collier's Year Book*. I keep up on such things. A few minutes ago I reviewed all my entries since 1978, and there is not one follow-up on the initial report.

This is not to say that the bishops have been doing nothing in the meantime. They have issued an extraordinary pastoral letter on nuclear arms; they are developing a vitally important pastoral on the American economic system; they are beginning to grapple with the issue of women in the Church, and one day will issue a pastoral letter on that subject too. There is nothing esoteric about these topics. The bishops are addressing questions that demand attention. But it would be the supreme irony if they produced sterling intellectual documents only to turn around and find the pews as underpopulated as ever. It could happen. The generations that the Church has always been able to presume in terms of loyalty, support and religious practice are thinning by the day as death makes its claims. There seems to be no impulse to fill the pews on the part of the new generations of adult Catholic Christians. All of which is to say that the Church must move to evangelize or activate, as the case may be, younger Catholics — not merely for the sake of souls, the salvation of souls being the Church's mission, but also for institutional survival. Ours is an enormous institutional entity, perhaps a top-heavy one. We feel the problems caused by the crisis in clerical vocations; we know what happened to parochial schools, at least in part because thousands of nuns opted for other ways of witness; we should be aware of what could happen to Church institutions across the board if the new generations of Catholics continue to drift away from interests hitherto supported financially and in personally apostolic ways.

And while the new generations of baptized Catholics are being evangelized, it might not be a bad idea to provide something akin to a continuing education for the older, more regular church-going Catholics. In his 1978 novel *The Human Factor*, Graham Greene sketches a scene of a well-dressed congregation, middle- and older-aged, standing at attention in song, their words issuing with a kind of defiance as though the worshippers inwardly doubted the facts: "There is a green hill far away, without a city wall." My recollection — my guess, really — is that it was a Catholic church; everything in Greene remains in a Catholic context, whatever his personal orthodoxy in the years since the "theological novels." In any instance, if it were not a Catholic church that Greene's Maurice Castle popped into, it could have been — in England or anywhere in the United States, for that matter.

I'm not a sociologist. I have not systematically surveyed the older generations of Catholics to seek to discover what they're believing these days. But, based on a variety of experiences, I would say that most are traveling on the old Baltimore Catechism, laced with the legalistic impulses mentioned earlier. To most older Catholics, Vatican Council II twenty-years-after seems to have devolved to a vernacular Mass and congregational singing (mumbled rather than engaged in with the defiance noted by Greene). Maybe that's better than nothing, the Mass being central to Catholic worship, but it isn't what Vatican II was nearly all about.

Maybe there's little point in saving the saved, but at the same time there may be a correlation between the indifference of the new generations and the simplisms (it seems such a harsh word) of the older generations about old truths and new Church. But whether there is or there is not, the Church owes more to its senior loyalists than indulgence of out-of-date pieties. Or pietisms, as the case may be.

Moving on, and speaking of "owing things," so much is owed to women by the Church that it is difficult to know precisely where to begin. There is the problem of sacramental discrimination, all seven sacraments being possible to men but only six to women, women being barred from Holy Orders by a chauvinist, latter-day application of the mores of the beginning of the Common Era. There is the problem of the Church's language, women being named what they are not — a brother, man — or not being named at all; or worse, being named in such a patronizing way — as in the counsels of St. Paul — as to stir the resentments of the half-sensitive person. There are structural injustices up and down the human scales of the Church, so real as to render women second-class members as a generic group. The anger of women over this situation has been manifested in dramatic ways in recent years, notably the 1979 incident in Washington when Mercy Sister M. Theresa Kane bluntly confronted Pope John Paul II on the equal role that should be women's "in all ministries of our Church."

Now I've mentioned the name of a sister, and I know that there are those who will say, almost by reflex: "Ah, another disgruntled nun. The Church would be a calmer place if it were not for peevish religious women." It's a leap to judgment that defies fairness and actualities. I don't know other people's experience, but mine is that dissatisfaction among Catholic women is not at all limited to sisters, or even to activist lay women (though sisters are technically lay persons, aren't they?). I sense a broad, quiet dissatisfaction in the Catholic family, which in not a few households has reversed the convention about which parent, which spouse is the regular churchgoer. Time was when invariably it was the woman. But that does not appear to be so uniformly the case anymore.

Take two women of my acquaintance. Once upon a time each was a regular at Mass, while the husbands —well, they were more casual. A Sunday golf date was more than sufficient reason to skip Mass. Or a late Saturday night. Or some chores about house or yard. But the wives would be in the pews. Now the situation is precisely the reverse. The husbands are regulars; the wives don't go to church at all, not even at Easter or Christmas. When I did my book on the New Nuns a few years ago,[2] I encountered a number of religious women who said they had virtually to force themselves to attend Mass, that it was insulting for a group of religious people living in a community to have to go outside their group in order to secure a person to preside at their central ceremony of communal worship. With these two female acquaintances, however, no ideology is at work, or at least no professed one. They're just not interested in Catholicism anymore. They're completely turned off, completely indifferent. Realize, these women went to parochial schools and sent their children to parochial schools. They were more than

[2]The New Nuns: Serving Where the Spirit Leads, by John Deedy, Fides/Claretian, Chicago, 1982.

merely formal Catholics. But then, just about the time
that the children were grown and making theirs individual decisions about the practice of their faith — all of
them irregularized — the mothers decided also to
irregularize.

Now Church leaders can get upset over assertive nuns,
but at least in their cases one knows what is bothering
them: the denial of Orders; the hamstringing of their
ability to witness; the problem of layers of paternalism
heaped upon them by male clerical structures in the
Church. When one knows the grievance, one can do
something about correcting the situation. But how does
one get at an indifference that seems rooted in nothing in
particular?

Admittedly I do not know how common my two
women acquaintances are. I go to church, look around,
and women dominate still in numbers. At the same time,
however, I am concerned that the indifference of my
friends might be a whole lot more widespread than
anyone presently suspects. For I see this indifference
among women demonstrated in a host of ways: the disin-
clination to be a part of parish guilds; the disinterest in
responding to appeals, as for CCD teachers (in my parish
most CCD teachers continue to be women, but the pastor
has almost to beg for them to come forth); the irreverent
response to religious exhortation from whatever source it
originates, be it pastor or pope. Which is not to say that
there are still not many women who are involved and
committed to whatever the Church wants; look at the
numbers of women active in the right-to-life movement.
On the other hand, however, there seems to be a growing
number who could care less about what the Church
thinks, wants or recommends. Are they obliquely resent-
ful for having been used as baby machines, or cake bakers,

or menders of the altar linens — people, in a word, who kept the cribs full and saw to menial jobs not expected of men? I have no idea, but those in leadership positions would be advised, it would seem, to find out before the indifference which is so common among young people leaps to or escalates among women.

Thus, in my opinion, perhaps the most important pastoral undertaking of the bishops in recent years is its letter on women in the Church, targeted for release in a year or two. The bishops have managed to have extraordinary impact, certainly in terms of the media, with their pastoral letters of recent years. The 1983 letter on nuclear arms is additionally thought to have had large impact on general public opinion —although this impact may be more authentically traced to serendipity than the pastoral itself. Certainly there has been a marked change of late in public attitudes towards nuclear weapons and the arms race, but how much due to the persuasiveness of the bishops and how much to the apparent dawning at last that nuclear war means Armageddon is a question. I imagine too that revelations about $500 ashtrays and that array of vastly overpriced "defense" materials have soured people on the whole business of arms.

But the impact of the nuclear-arms pastoral — how direct, how oblique? — is incidental to the discussion at hand. What is not irrelevant — in fact it's downright sad — is that the bishops are likely to find that they had much more latitude, much more freedom from Rome (oversight notwithstanding) in drawing up their nuclear-arms pastoral and again in proceeding about their pastoral on justice and the American economic system than they will have in composing their pastoral letter on women. Here, so many inhibitions will be at work on the bishops, inhibitions born of two-thousand years of history and centuries of conventions. There is the anomaly, for instance, that even as this essay is written, many dioceses of the United States cannot decide whether the new Code of Canon Law opens the sanctuary gate to "altar girls," since the new Code does not make specific mention of a prohibition against "women approaching the altar" as did the 1917 Code. The permission not being spelled out, the policy of most, if not all dioceses is not to make an aggressive pro-feminist reading of possibilities opened up, but to cautiously settle that the controlling norm is in the directive of the Holy See, *Inestimabile Donum*, which prohibits female altar servers. One diocese — Worcester, Massachusetts — has gone further and declared that even to encourage female altar servers at this time "does a very practical disservice to the Christian community in a pastoral sense," the contention being that respect for the law of the Church is basic to pastoral practice and disregarding the law "often leads to the imposition of one's own will in place of the law, upon others" and then to "destructive confrontation." Say what one wants about such a rationale, but it makes one thing clear. Large difficulty lies ahead for meaningful dialogue on the role of women in the Church, when so minor an issue as "altar girls" provokes so tortured an exercise as Worcester's. What can one expect when the subject moves to more substantive questions, like women in the Permanent Diaconate or women in the priesthood itself? It is not easy to be optimistic.

But optimistic we must be, for to be otherwise is to risk cynicism, despair, hopelessness, and to default on the moral support that Catholics should furnish their bishops — as the bishops themselves should provide the leadership which merits that support. It's not a one-way street. In recent years, and again thanks in no small part to the nuclear-arms pastoral letter, the bishops have recovered some of the credibility that had slipped down the drain in 1968, continuing into the 1970s (O, *Humanae Vitae*; O, Vietnam). Credibility is back, at least partly, but every bit of it is on the line now as Catholics look beyond the forthcoming economics pastoral to that on women in the Church. The bishops must perform, or chance the alienation of half their members; to say nothing of those males who are comrades in cause; and to say nothing of the younger generations, who to be evangelized must have people as well as doctrine in which to believe.

Thus to summarize the promises and the urgencies of the '80s: The bishops have to make good on their 1978 promise to evangelize the unchurched, which means, among other things, evangelizing those American Catholics of the younger generations who have taken a walk; second, the bishops must help Catholic women to realize at last the promise which is theirs as members of a Church which in the ideal knows no sexist sub-divisions.

The Laity and Alienated Catholics

Sidney Callahan

Laypersons in the American Catholic Church come in many more varieties than one supposes. If there ever existed the monolithic phalanx feared in paranoiac fantasies, the ranks have broken. Today there exist multitudes of diverse lay groups displaying different ideologies and various styles of life and worship. There are the conservative laity committed to Romanitas and pre-Vatican II thought and worship. There are middle of the road types living out the revolution wrought by Vatican II, side by side with more daring experimental groups living out their vision of the future Church. Finally, there are those baptized Catholics beyond the pale— dropped out, alienated, missing in action. I am most interested in the alienated, since I live among them; but before entering this troubled territory, attention must be paid to the good news. Thousands upon thousands of lively Roman Catholic layfolk are deeply involved in their faith anywhere and everywhere you might go in the United States of America.

And where are most of the laity located if we were scanning an imaginary ideological map? It's difficult to be sure, but my impression is that most of the flourishing laity are mainly found in the ideological center, despite the disproportionate noise, trouble and political clout in Rome exercised by ultra-conservative rightwing Catholics. Most Americn Catholics take naturally to Vatican II's vision of an ever-reforming Church, and so have welcomed change. In this new vision of the Church as the people of God, laypersons no longer think of themselves as some subsidiary arm of the Church militant, whose secret mission is to penetrate the world in order to bring about the triumph of Roman Catholicism. Now laypeople think of themselves as *being* the Church in the world.

In fact, laypersons hardly think of themselves as "the laity" anymore. The old fashioned term calls to mind the old sharp distinctions between clergy and laity, a distinction which is fast breaking down. Just as the boundary between the Church and the world has become less distinct, so has the distinction between priest and layperson. The old clerical culture, the old clerical mystique no longer invokes the old awe or automatic authority. Priests don't have to work at modestly reminding their parishioners that they are as other men; it is all too obviously true. Maybe the flood of priests who left in the 60's and 70's helped demystify the vocation. Or perhaps the increasing education, competence and commitment of the laity has erased the distinctions which used to exist in an immigrant Church.

At any rate, the laypersons' conviction of "being a royal priesthood" each and everyone called to serve, has grown. Christ's work has to be done, the world has to be loved and transformed; various people are called to various ministries. Christians work together in teams where it is no longer an issue who is ordained and who is not. Leadership is where you find it, as the Holy Spirit seems intent on proving generation after generation. This generation of active American Catholics seems to have heard the gospel message and they don't wait around for a priest to lead them. Surely the resulting panoply of good works and devotion must gladden the heart of God, as well as the American Bishops.

Less delightful to the Bishops may be the fact that when there arise irresolvable conflicts between laypeople and the clergy, layfolk often just detach themselves and go on about their work, in various versions of the end run. Even the rightwing conservatives think nothing of solving *their* problems by running to Rome to curtail liberal clergy. Ironically, the people in the American Church who now must suffer unjust authoritarian strictures are the clergy and religious, especially of course, religious women. When is the last time you have heard of any layperson threatened with ecclesiastical sanction? Happily, the majority of American laypeople can sing along with Anna in the "King and I," "I'm a free and independent employee," certainly no slave who must kowtow to the King.

Unfortunately, the old monarchical model of the Church still seems to flourish in Rome. Pope John Paul II reigns in a very authoritarian way, only with more attractiveness and charisma than his predecessors. My own explanation of John Paul's rule is to look back to his formation under the German occupation. If you grow up under the Gestapo the ready model of Church you get is that of an underground guerilla organization. In the underground, absolute obedience, conformity, authoritarian command, and tight unity are necessary. Domestic life, women, diversity, and democratic processes may weaken the fighting unit and so are sacrificed for the duration. If an underground mentality is united to an existentialist philosophy of choice and the need to risk all against the background of death and suffering, there will emerge a very romantic exalted view of priesthood, women, sex, and daily Christian life. Romantic heroic standards have to be held high by an elite; the high ground justifies highhandedness and a reluctance to loosen central control.

Many in the American Church, laity and clergy, are offended by the present regression to authoritarianism in the name of authority. Struggles are going on, and will continue to go on over the rights of Catholics (even Bishops) in the Church. My own view of the ideal function of Church authority is modelled on the way authority operates in science. Or given the history of science's emergence in the West, we should perhaps say that Greco-Judeo-Christian thought took a view of Divine authority which influenced the emergence and advancement of science. The work of science is founded on the assumption that Truth or lawful reality exists and that human inquiry can succeed in constructing better and better approximations or models of that Truth. The basis of scientific method is an exemplary effort of humans not to fool themselves (just as in the spiritual life). Reason and perseverance produces cumulative findings which are constructed, and reconstructed, as models of Reality.

When a mistaken or inadequate model of reality has been constructed, things gradually start going wrong and new evidence arises which doesn't fit the picture. Signals from reality start revealing the old model's inappropriateness. Then there ensues a painful process of struggle and reconstruction. But the scientific authority which decides whether the new model is a better construction, is a collegial group of the best scientists who have dedicated themselves to their discipline, and been acknowledged as the most insightful in their search. The freedom to seek truth which they have enjoyed, and the dedication to truth employed in the struggle, means that the final consensus of the scientific community is uncoerced. Whenever a Commissar, or Inquisitor, or censor interferes in an effort to impose a scientific party line in a disputed question, science stops progressing.

In the Church a similar process seems to take place. The best interpreters of the tradition, guided we believe by the Holy Spirit, form a living ongoing collegial community which shares in a consensus about God's revealed Truth. When challenges come from outside, the community consults on its understanding of truth. When challenged by internal struggles over either the content of revelation, or the processes of communal decision making, the Church goes through a more painful process. Which contending party within best reflects the reality of God's will and the Gospel of the Risen Lord? If there is freedom of inquiry, the best members of the community of seekers of truth will persuade the whole group, just as scientists persuade the scientific community to reconstruct its model of reality.

Occasionally, in science and in the Church, a party neither persuades nor is persuaded and is inevitably separated from the ongoing community consensus. After full hearing of claims and counterclaims, and long processes of testing, the collegial community of the best practitioners consult and decide with the authority of the community. In today's scientific community, for instance, the claims of astrology and phrenology have been decisively rejected. In the Church, a host of beliefs and practices have also been rejected: the acceptability of slavery, the need for Kings, the toleration of racism, the use of torture in the Inquistion, and so on.

In most processes of change or development in the Church three constituencies can be discerned at work: the theologians and scholars, the hierarchy, and the laity. If two out of the three agree, change occurs. If only one constituency is persuaded without the other two, nothing happens. This process is quite evident in the birth control controversy, when you have the Pope and much of the hierarchy proscribing artificial birth control, while almost all the laity and theologians have accepted it as consonant with God's will for Christians. In other disputed matters such as accepting married men or women as priests, no two constituencies have been able to coalesce. Thus as Newman so adroitly argued a full century ago, the laity can make a mighty difference in how the Church goes in any particular era. Every authority must be accorded attention and assent before it can have force or enforce. The American Bishops exercise authority only if the American laity and theologians listen and support them. The Pope will have authority only if his fellow Bishops, the Church's theologians and the laity support him.

These problems of authority within the Church and the ongoing struggle over Church structures and the content of the Gospel may seem abstract, but they do impinge on the daily life of the laity. The liveliness of the involved laypersons going about Christian ministry has been the first fruits of the reform and revisioning of Church. Lay-people accorded full membership by theologians and Bishops, take responsibility in new ways; they act like adults instead of children. Slowly the adolescent American Church is growing up.

But what of those who have dropped out and left already? Have they been lost for good? Why do they leave when others stay? Within the last several decades many of those born and brought up as American Roman Catholics ceased the practice of the faith. People have always left the Catholic Church, but such a huge exodus in such a short time provokes a thirst for explanations. When the ultimate research project gets around to investigating this recent phenomenon, what intuitions or typology of alien-ation might be useful in shaping the inquiry? Admittedly, for me this is not just an interesting abstract question, since sometimes it seems that everyone I know and love who once was a Catholic, now is not, or not so as you'd notice.

Looking at the people I've known and observing the rest of the present scene I think you can construct a worst case and best case scenario, with large groups ambigu-ously located somewhere on the middle of the continuum. The worst case version of today's lapsed Catholic has little to do with those stories depicted in old time retreat preaching, now so upstaged by the Fundamentalist Prot-estants. In this simple-minded approach, leaving the Church is equated with apostasy and is motivated by the evil wish to sin and slothfully backslide without a care. The lapsed Catholic wants the Devil's worldly gains which the Church refuses to condone: contraceptives, abortions, divorces, adulteries, ill-gotten fortune, or assimilation into the Wasp ascendancy or secular intellectual elite.

This worst case is far too dramatic, and fairly optimistic, since such flaming sinners so often come round to romantic conversions, deep repentance or at least deathbed reconciliations. My own worst case of the alienated Catholic is much more pessimistic and decidedly cooler. I think William James is correct when he describes some personalities as being inherently, temperamentally non-religious. They are "either incapable of imagining the invisible; or else, in the language of devotion, they are life-long subjects of 'barrenness' and 'dryness.' " Either through an intellectual conviction of materialism, or frozen, inhibited energies, they can never be active believers. It is as if they are religiously tone deaf. They do not "get it," or begin to comprehend what believers experience or are exercised about.

In an earlier, less pluralistic society, with severe sanctions upon unbelievers, these people would in all probability continue to conform in externals. Their bodies might fill the pews, but their central selves would remain untouched. As long as external sanctions were in operation, they would perform their religious duty. But once an inner assent or spiritual participation is expected they are lost. Ironically, the reforms of Vatican II can bring about the "spiritualizing" of the Church which lets them leave. That, and the fact that in America it is now socially acceptable to lapse or choose some other "lifestyle." Now that Catholics are assimilated and no longer a persecuted minority, they do not even need the old tribal loyalty which encouraged conformity. These religiously tone-deaf persons may be good people, even moral people, but they are not going to be returning to the Church.

My best case scenario of alienation involves those persons who become so intensely spiritual that they leave what they see as the confinement of the Roman Catholic Church and become Quakers or Zen Buddhists or join some other transcendental faith or philosophy. It is not so much that they totally reject their heritage, they just feel that they have expanded beyond the Christian Incarnation and must be more inclusive. They would demand more mystical meditation and openness for themselves than the traditional western approach to religious life can give. Catholicism with its rationality, compromises, historical baggage and institutional life is just not intense or pure enough for them. They soar right out of the ordinary parish and probably won't be back.

Then there are the alienated laypeople who are somewhere in between the tone deaf and the transcendental mystics. They have dropped out because of some combination of factors. They can be best understood by meditating on what *keeps* a person practicing a religion. Here again William James is a reliable guide when he says that a viable religion must be "philosophically reasonable," "morally helpful," and "immediately luminous." Gordon Allport, another psychologist interested in religion, reiterates these judgments when he says that one's religion must be "morally true" as well as "metaphysically true." Neither James nor Allport sees the origin of religious faith as significant; they both assert that whatever the genesis of belief in the past (fear, love, social conditioning), it is the ongoing present experience and meanings of religious practice which validate the religious life. To these comments, I would add my own observation that the religion must also provide some community, some social world, in which support and altruistic action is possible. Often the baptized Catholics who now are missing in action have missed some of the necessary conditions for faith.

Often the need for philosophical reasonableness has been violated by a rotten Catholic education or some equally narrow secular indoctrination in old-fashioned scientific positivism. To rectify either or both inadequacies, can solve this problem. To my mind there's never been an era in which theology, science, and the intellectual life have been more theoretically compatible. All the old bugaboos have been disarmed by scriptural scholarship and scientific progress. But if the requirement of philosophical reasonableness is no longer a difficulty, the need for moral helpfulness, immediate luminosity and community remain problematic.

The Church's ability to be morally helpful to the modern American laity has often been inhibited by distortions of Christian teaching on (what else?) sex and power. Many women, in particular are alienated by the remnants of some combination of feminine mystique and misogyny which ends up not only banning contraception, but excluding women from ordination and other critical leadership positions. Problems in accepting sexuality and accepting women seem to be alike. The ban on married priests and the imposition of mandatory celibacy spring from these same Manichaean clouds, still wafting about in the western Church. Needless to say, homosexual Catholics or divorced Catholics, are equally stigmatized. In matters of sexuality, many Catholics have not found the Church morally helpful, instead they have found it needlessly cruel and destructive. Many of the middle-aged missing are still bitter over the birth control wars, and what they see as a betrayal inflicted in their formative years.

Moreover, power has not been exercised in a just way within the Church, and this too has inhibited the moral helpfulness of the Church for many. Without democratic due process and fair practice, the institution has been flawed. Today, the American Church's growing consciousness of the need for peace and justice is a marvelous witness of the Spirit. But these new movements toward moral leadership may again founder if justice is not exercised within the Church. A community must exist in which all members can give as adults give, and get support and validation. Lucky are those laypersons in the Church who when frozen out in the local parish, are able to find larger national Catholic groups providing the social support they need. The list of potential Catholic communities is long and diverse: charismatic Catholics, Commonweal Catholics, third orders, Catholic Worker communities, the Ladies of Charity, the Catholic Family Movement, labor organizations, the Legion of Mary, Cursillos, Pax Christi, and so on. A person of every temperament, every intellectual level, and almost every ideology may find a home *if* they deem the search worthwhile.

The worthwhileness of the effort arises from that most mysterious of William James' requirements: immediate luminousness. Does one experience an inner validation of God's presence and love? It seems this experience of luminousness can be helped along by good liturgy. Part of our present problem as a Church is the evolution of a new liturgy or liturgies, which can do for us now what the Tridentine mass did for its time. But even while we fumble around liturgically, some religious experiences carry their own authorization and illumination of truth. This is as real as anything else I know, and the whole of me knows it. I may not be able "to prove it" to others, but I know this reality leads me to God's Truth and Love. Such religious experiences may happen much more frequently for more people than we suppose. Otherwise why do people persevere through so much worship and religious life that outwardly looks so disappointing? The light may come and go, the sense of God's reality blows hot or cold, but I cannot give up the incontrovertible experience of the Sun's (or Son's) rays once felt. From time to time, our hearts burn within us, and the dross is burned away. So we stay in the Church; and sometimes those who leave come back.

I think that many of the more mildly alienated Catholic laity may eventually swell the ranks of the returnees. Once reform has penetrated further and adult re-education has taken place, our members missing in action may begin to straggle back. Our youngish, mobile, educated urban careerists even now show signs of serious re-evaluation of priorities. The mystique of the career world of upward mobility and material consumption seems to be fading. Other moral visions will have a chance. Surely, the Catholic Church will have a chance. Recently I overheard two fine lapsed Catholics in their twenties in a rather telling dialogue. Said one when describing his religious state; "Yes, I'm an atheist, but you have to understand, I'm a *Catholic* atheist." The other young man, in reply to an inquiry about his recent encounter with the Moonies, laughed and said, "No, of course I wasn't attracted; after all when I'm ready, I have the Catholic Church waiting for me." Well, let's hope so.

Whatever happens, this American Church of the 80's that is ready and waiting, is a Church being shaped by laypeople. If, as seems likely, this is a time of crisis, and another turning point in the long pilgrimage of Catholics, then American Catholic laypeople are crucially involved in determining which road will be taken. Christ's Peace, Justice, Love and Liberty may be born anew, here and now in America, the land of the free. Why not? With God, nothing is impossible.

American Catholicism and the Biblical Movement

~ ❋ ~

Donald Senior, C.P.
Carroll Stuhlmueller, C.P.

It would be possible to chart the issues and style of the biblical movement in the American Catholic church of today by simply running one's finger down a shelf of some recent Orbis publications on biblical topics.

Christology at the Crossroads.

God of the Lowly: Socio-Historical Interpretations of the Bible.

Spirituality of the Beatitudes: Matthew's Challenge for First World Christians.

The Way to Peace: Liberation Through the Bible.

Political Issues in Luke-Acts.

My Enemy is My Guest: Jesus and Violence in Luke-Acts.

Jesus the Stranger: Homilies for the A Cycle.

The Biblical Foundations for Mission.

Materialist Approaches to the Bible.

The Gospel According to Solentiname.

Even though many of these titles were not written by American authors (or even Roman Catholic ones), their subject matter reflects new and important currents in biblical studies and ones typical of the mood of American Catholicism in the 1980's. Each of them blends substantial theological and exegetical issues with pressing pastoral concerns. Each of them wrestles with questions that are at once global and truly "catholic" and yet have a particular connection with or challenge to American culture.

In several instances Orbis publications have been on the cutting edge of new methodologies, especially those drawn from the positive sciences. The work of Norman Gottwald, *The Tribes of Yahweh*, and that of Willy Schottroff and Wolfgang Stegemann, *The God of the Lowly*, each of which applies sociological and political models to the biblical data, would be good examples. Collaboration with the positive sciences in biblical and theological studies, while not a preserve of American exegesis, is becoming an important part of its distinctive contribution to biblical scholarship.

Much of the credit for the way Orbis Books has kept in tune with the biblical currents of American Catholicism belongs to the gracious, perceptive and extraordinary American Catholic honored in this volume. Philip Scharper and Orbis Books recognized the issues—in biblical studies as well as in the many other facets of church life reflected on by the authors in this volume.

Our own attempt to step back and survey the current state of American Catholicism in the area of biblical studies will take its cue from the Orbis shelf. The qualities that best characterize the Catholic biblical movement in this country are: a vigorous blend of scientific scholarship and pastoral interest, wide popular impact, and significant ecumenical collaboration. We will attempt to illustrate this by first tracing briefly the history of the biblical movement in the United States, especially under the aegis of the Catholic Biblical Association of America. We then assess the implementation of Vatican II in the area of biblical studies. Here, as in everything else, the American church was profoundly influenced by the directives and spirit of the Council. To a remarkable degree, the pastoral recommendations found in the Council's document on Revelation (*Dei Verbum*) have charted the direction taken by the biblical movement in this country. Finally, we will take a look at the crucial areas of popular piety and ecumenism—two arenas in which the impact of the biblical renewal has been particularly strong.

The Catholic Biblical Association of America

While the Catholic Biblical Association (hereafter, CBA) is organized as a community of scholars, it was a pastoral impulse that brought it into existence. Archbishop Edwin V. O'Hara, at first of the diocese of Great Falls, MT (1930-39) and then of the diocese of Kansas City-St. Joseph, MO (1939-56) chaired the American bishops' Committee of the Confraternity of Christian Doctrine (hereafter, CCD). To strengthen and enrich the catechetical instruction of youth and to achieve more effective preaching and adult discussion, he saw the need of a new English translation of the Bible. On the 18th of January 1936 he convened a meeting of Catholic biblical scholars in Washington, D.C.; Fr. Romain Butin, C.M., proposed that plans be enlarged to include a permanent society of Catholic scholars. This proposal was imple-

mented in New York during the second national catechetical congress of the CCD, 3 January 1936, at which Fr.
Edward P. Arbez, S.S., presided.

The first general meeting of the CBA convened a year
later, 9-10 October 1937, and adopted a constitution. Its
goals and purpose state explicitly the pastoral intent of the
association: 1) to "place at the disposal of the Episcopal
committee of CCD a body of men qualified for the inves-
tigation of biblical problems"; 2) to "promote mutual
acquaintance among Catholic scholars of America"; and
3) a goal added and ratified only in 1952, to "devote itself
to the scientific study of the Bible . . . in conformity with
the spirit and the instructions of the Catholic Church."

Tensions between scholarship and popularization
began to surface during the early years of the CBA.
Gradually the CBA was holding its meetings separately
from those of the CCD. Some of the older members still
recall the faithful attendance of Archbishop O'Hara, pre-
siding at the main table but catching up with lost sleep as
the presentations became ever more technical. Yet scholarship for the sake of the apostolate continued vigorously.
Members of the CBA were busily at work preparing a
new English translation from the Latin Vulgate, the official text of the Roman Catholic church until the encyclical of Pope Pius XII, *Divino Afflante Spiritu*, called for
translations from the original languages. Although issued
30 September 1943, the feast of St. Jerome, its contents did
not reach the USA until the first month of 1944. On 22
April 1944 seven years of work on the Latin Vulgate were
abandoned; God alone knows how many tears first
dropped on the pages of that meticulous work before they
were confined to the circular file.

Plans immediately got underway for what was to

become *The New American Bible*. The translation was originally called the Confraternity version. Volume 1, Genesis to
Ruth, was published in 1952; Vol 3, Job to Sirach, in 1955;
Vol 4, Isaia to Malachia, in 1961, and finally Vol 2, Samuel
to Maccabees, in 1969. By the time the final volume was
ready, some significant changes came about. The spelling
of proper names (Isaia in the Confraternity version
instead of Isaias used in former Rheims-Douay version)
was made to conform to that common in the English
language: i.e., Isaiah, Malachi. Material from the Dead
Sea Scrolls was used particularly in the second volume.
Protestant scholars helped in revising Volume 1. The
name, as already mentioned, was changed to *The New
American Bible*.

Clearer lines were drawn between the scientific purpose of the CBA and its involvement in the popularization
of the Bible by inaugurating a new magazine, *The Bible
Today*.

Other significant developments were happening in the
CBA. In 1947 the first woman became a full active
member, Mother Kathryn Sullivan of the Religious of the
Sacred Heart. She was to labor prodigiously with Monsignor John E. Steinmueller of the Brooklyn diocese (who
incidentally with Fr. Charles J. Callan, O.P. was the first
American consultor of the Pontifical Biblical Commission, 1947-71) in producing the first wave of Catholic
textbooks for colleges and seminaries, *Companion to the
New Testament* (1945) and *Catholic Biblical Encyclopedia*
(1950). She directed the audio-visual department of the
CBA (1948-70) and prepared the first three decennial
indexes of *The Catholic Biblical Quarterly* (1948, 58, 68).
During 1958-59 Kathryn Sullivan was vice-president of
the CBA.

A maturing of an ecumenical spirit can also be seen. While William Foxwell Albright had already been voted an honorary member in 1944 and observer exchange had been taking place with the Society of Biblical Literature since 1959, active membership was formally opened to non-Catholics only in 1962. Paul J. Achtemeier would become the first Protestant to be voted president of the CBA, 1984-85.

"Unless the grain of wheat falls to the earth and dies..." (John 12:24)—suffering is always the biblical way to new and stronger life. The CBA was led along this painful path during the years immediately before the opening of the Second Vatican Council. Some of these details are chronicled for us in a history of the CBA, prepared as a presidential address by Monsignor Francis S. Rossiter and published in a Supplement to *The Catholic Biblical Quarterly* 39 (July 1977) 1-14; these and other details of this chapter are drawn from this source. In 1961 the Holy Office issued a warning against those scholars who questioned the "germane historical and objective truth not only of the Old Testament but also of the New Testament, even the very words and deeds of Jesus Christ" and so were responsible for disturbing the conscience of the faithful (*Osservatore Romano,* 22 June 1961). Along with the articles of Ernesto Cardinal Ruffini this *Monitum* was interpreted as a condemnation of form criticism and historical criticism. To cooperate with the intent of these instructions, the Cincinnati national assembly of the CBA voted that "the general meetings of the CBA will be closed meetings for the active members exclusively." This decision of the executive committee was amended, through the intervention of another pioneer scholar of the association, Msgr. Patrick W. Skehan, "the

President is empowered to invite individual non-active members..." (*CBQ* 23 [1961] 468-9). Those who attended this meeting vouch for the vigor of the discussion, the pain on the faces of such faithful and serious Catholics as Msgr. Skehan, and the equal determination to remain faithful to biblical scholarship.

One person who bore the brunt of attack and criticism was Fr. Edward F. Siegman, C.PP.S., editor of the *CBQ* between 1951-58. In the national meeting of 1962, held at Maryknoll, NY with the blessing of Cardinal Spellman, the resolution of Msgr. Patrick W. Skehan was passed unanimously: "the membership of the CBA assembled in its annual meeting wish to convey to Rev. Edward F. Siegman, C.PP.S., their fraternal sympathy in his present anxieties and to assure him of their earnest good wishes and their prayers" (*CBQ* 24 [1964] 424). Fr. Siegman died of a second heart attack, many think as a martyr to the cause of biblical scholarship, 2 February 1967, while president of the CBA. As late as 1969 the CBA felt obliged to vote a resolution, urging due process for any beleaguered members. Attacks from the right have continued, particularly against such members of the CBA as Fr. Raymond E. Brown, S.S.

Many accomplishments of the CBA have already been recorded here. Many others have been passed over because of the limitations of space. The association has grown from the initial one hundred charter active members in 1937, all ordained priests in the Roman Catholic church, to the more than 800 active members in 1984, composed of diocesan priests and members of religious orders, male and female, lay persons, Catholic, Protestant and Jewish. The large majority remain Roman Catholic and the goal of the CBA is still to "devote itself to the scientific study of the Bible ... in conformity with the spirit and the instructions of the Catholic Church." The pastoral and spiritual ambience of the scientific study of the Bible, however, shows up in many ways at the national meeting and in the work of the membership. The national meeting is normally held with budget economy at seminaries, and religious colleges or universities; daily eucharistic liturgies and Bible services remain in the program of activities. The income of the association, gained through royalties from *The New American Bible*, is annually tithed for donations to the poor. Financial aid has been voted for visiting professors at the Pontifical Biblical Institute, Rome, and the Ecole Biblique et Archaeologique, Jerusalem. Each year a grant has been given to such enterprises as the new translation of the Bible into Japanese under the direction of Fr. Bernardin V. Schneider, O.F.M., Tokyo. Task forces and continuing seminars at the annual meeting include such a range of topics as the ministerial role of women according to the New Testament, the social foundations of peace from biblical perspectives, etc. Again we meet the blend of contemporary pastoral questions with scientific biblical study.

Vatican II and the Catholic Biblical Movement in America

As already pointed out, the charter document that breathed new life into Catholic biblical scholarship was Pius XII's 1943 encyclical *Divino Afflante Spiritu*. But the creative forces set in motion by this act of liberation were able to struggle to their feet (and not without some continuing skirmishes with reactionary church authority) and burst into the clear with the declaration of the Council. Vatican II's Dogmatic Constitution on Divine Revelation (*Dei Verbum*) was, like most of the Council's texts, a compromise document, keeping strong links to past formulations on such issues as the nature of inspiration, biblical inerrancy, and the relationship between Scripture and tradition. But at the same time it provided sufficient latitude for biblical exegesis to pursue its work with integrity. It is not an exaggeration to say that the American Catholic church took the Council's strong endorsement of the biblical renewal with full seriousness, and in the course of a generation had moved from a position of weakness to one of vigorous strength.

In a chapter entitled, "Sacred Scripture in the Life of the Church," the Dogmatic Constitution on Divine Revelation or *Dei Verbum* concluded with a series of pastoral directives which now seem like a preview of the biblical movement in this country. Taking the recommendations in order, we can point to their impact on Catholic experience.

The first may be the most problematic. Because the church is to be nourished "at the one table of the Word of God and the Body of Christ" (par #21), the Council recommended that a crucial area of renewal should be preaching: ". . . all the preaching of the Church, as indeed the entire Christian religion, should be nourished and ruled by sacred Scripture" (par #21).

While the American church has a long way to go in fulfilling that mandate, it is remarkable to consider how far it has come. The quality of Catholic preaching in this country is quite uneven, as both laity and clergy themselves recognize. But there is no question that it has been profoundly influenced by the biblical movement. Any diocesan director of continuing education will testify that biblical topics—particularly if linked to the preaching ministry—are perennially at the top of the list when America Catholic clergy are asked for their preferences in opportunities for updating. Workshops on preaching, involving whole dioceses or state conferences, continue to draw significant enrollment. Homily preparation aids have multiplied in the past twenty years and the most successful ones, such as *Celebration*, *Weekday Homily Helps* or *Scripture in the Church*, have substantial material on the biblical background of the Lectionary selections. Periodicals that have priests and deacons as their major audience inevitably include features on preaching and the Bible.

A critical area is that of homiletic training in the seminaries and theological schools. While here, too, there has been significant improvement, homiletics remain an amazingly peripheral concern in many American seminaries. Liturgical preaching is and will remain for the foreseeable future the single most important encounter that the average Catholic will have with biblical interpretation. But whatever assessment one makes of the quality of preaching in the American Catholic church, there is no question that the quest to make it more biblical has become firmly rooted.

If one takes "preaching" in a wider sense, the impact of the biblical renewal is even more apparent. For example, no significant church document on theological or pastoral questions issued by a local ordinary or by the entire conference of United States Bishops could now afford to appear without a solid consideration of the biblical aspects of the question. This is, of course, a characteristic of post-Vatican II theology as a whole. But there has been fruitful collaboration between the American Bishops and Catholic biblical scholarship in the production of their two most famous statements on nuclear warfare and on the U.S. economy. Both the final version of *The Challenge to Peace* and the initial drafts of the statement on the economy base their pastoral reflections on an extensive biblical foundation. As a number of scholars have suggested, more formal utilization of the CBA in the preparation of such major statements might be worth consideration, but at the very least no one could accuse the bishop of ignoring their own conciliar directive that "preaching" should be "nourished and ruled by sacred Scripture" (*Dei Verbum* #21).

Other pastoral recommendations from the Council have had more uniform success. Because "access to sacred Scripture ought to be open wide to the Christian faithful" (par #22), the Council reiterated the directives of Pope Pius XII's encyclical, *Divino Afflante Spiritu*, that translations be made into the vernacular languages, not from the Latin Vulgate text as in the past, but from the original biblical languages. It further recommended that, if possible, this be done as a "joint effort with the separated brethren" (par #22). (We will comment on the ecumenical dimensions of the biblical movement later on).

Several principles that have driven the biblical movement in this country are found in this paragraph. Most fundamental of all is the basic tenet that access to Scripture should be "open wide" to all Christians. For a church that in practice (more than in principle) often rationed access to the Bible, such a conciliar mandate was revolutionary. And, as the Council suggested, one of the basic means of providing access is solid and available translations. As already indicated above, a major project of the post-Vatican II Church was *The New American Bible*. Although its quality, particularly in the New Testament

sections, received mixed reviews, this version ranks as one
of the most important and widely disseminated translations in the English-speaking world. The ability of American Catholic scholarship to mount such a project was a
sign of its coming of age. A thorough revision of this
translation is now being completed; the number of American Catholic biblical scholars able to be called upon for
the revision far exceeds the number available when the
project first began—another sign of the maturation of
biblical scholarship in this country.

The expanding pool of biblical scholars in the American church was itself in accord with another directive of
the Council text. Because interpretation of the Bible was
understood to be such an essential quality of authentic
Christian teaching, the Council gave a thumping endorsement to a deeper integration of Scripture into every
aspect of the church's teaching and recommended that the
pool of biblical scholarship be expanded. " 'Study of the
sacred page' should be the very soul of sacred theology"
(par #24). Every dimension of the church's ministry—
preaching, catechetics and "all forms of Christian
instruction"—was to be based on Scripture (par #24). All
"priests...deacons or catechists" were asked to
"immerse themselves in the Scriptures by constant sacred
reading and diligent study" (par #25).

The "Christian faithful" were not ignored. Quoting
Jerome the Council reminded the laity that "ignorance of
the Scriptures is ignorance of Christ" (par #25) and urged
them to "go to the sacred text itself," whether in the
context of the liturgy or other settings where reflection
on the Scripture was made available.

It would be naive to suggest that the entire American
church has been inflamed with biblical study since the

Council. But anyone familiar with the church scene can testify to the extraordinary interest in biblical courses and workshops that continues unabated in the American church.

Perhaps a special sign of this is the phenomenon of summer workshops. In addition to long-standing summer school programs that have a strong biblical component (for example, the University of San Francisco, Loyola Pastoral Institute of Chicago or Boston College), there are a number of biblical seminars that sprung into life immediately after the Council and have continued to draw from across the country hundreds of laity, deacons, priests and religious each year. Some long-running examples would be the Georgetown institute directed by Joseph Fitzmyer, S.J., the Trinity College institute directed by Miriam Ward, R.S.M., the College Misericordia institute inaugurated by Marianna Gildea, R.S.M. and now directed by Noel Keller, R.S.M., the Sinsinawa Bible Institute directed for many years by Helen O'Neil, O.P., and the Chicago Summer Scripture Seminar under the direction of Fr. Wayne Prist and Dr. Dolores Nicosia of the Center for Pastoral Ministry. Despite the staggering number of workshops and seminars on various topics offered each year in this country (the Spring listings in the *National Catholic Reporter* have become an annual ritual) the biblical ones run on unabated. New major institutes join the ranks each year such as those in Denver, Greenville, SC, Buffalo, and San Antonio, to name a few.

The mix of biblical scholars, clergy, religious and laity that characterizes these institutes are, we believe, a special sign of hope for the future of the American church and surely an indicator of phenomenal interest in the Bible. That same interest can be found on the parish and diocesan level. In a majority of American parishes it is routine to find at least a small corps of Bible study or prayer groups, something virtually unheard of in a Catholic setting twenty years ago. Many dioceses conduct special Bible study programs or institutes.

An important ingredient in this biblical movement has been the growing band of American Catholic scholars. In the years immediately following the Council numerous dioceses and religious orders of men sent candidates for the licentiate and doctorate in Scripture to the European centers of Rome (the Pontifical Biblical Institute), Louvain, Paris, and some German universities, as well as the Ecole Biblique in Jerusalem. With the exception of Catholic University in Washington, DC and its strong Semitics department, there were no Catholic graduate schools available in America. Graduates from these classic continental centers eventually joined the ranks of American Catholic scholars who were already on the scene when the Council arrived. The green light flashed by Pius XII in *Divino Afflante Spiritu* had enabled scholars already in the field to be freer in publishing the results of their research and encouraged many ordinaries and religious superiors to send men on for graduate work in Scripture. Armed with new critical methodologies, these "pioneers" were making their mark on the American scene even before the advent of the Council. Although it is risky to quote names for fear of missing many, some of those who belong in this pantheon would have to be such people as Barnabas Ahern, Myles Bourke, John L. McKenzie, Raymond Brown, Joseph Fitzmyer, Louis Hartman, George MacRae, Eugene Maly, Roland Murphy, Patrick Skehan, Gerard Sloyan, Bruce Vawter.

In the past few years this scene has shifted to some

degree. The tide of fresh biblical scholarship continues but it is no longer an exclusively clerical tide. The membership list of the CBA now includes lay people and significant numbers of women religious. Each year their active participation in teaching and publications grows. And no longer do aspiring biblical scholars turn only to European centers for their training. A majority of candidates look to programs at Yale, Harvard, Princeton, Chicago, Vanderbilt and Berkeley and other universities. Although a few solid masters programs are in place, American Catholicism has not yet produced a doctoral program in biblical studies on a par with its Protestant and secular counterparts (however, solid efforts are being made at Catholic University and Marquette).

The diversity of American Catholic biblical scholarship (lay and clerical, male and female, European and American-trained) is one of its (often unacknowledged) strengths, as it is of the American church in general. Although the danger of cacophony is not absent, such cross-fertilization blends a continental focus on the classic methods of form, source and redaction criticism, with the American interest in literary criticism and sociological methodologies, and has led to a broader and fresher interpretation of the text. The addition of women to the Catholic biblical guild has also opened new perspectives, most important of which is a feminist reading of the biblical texts. One of the most notable contributions in this field has been *In Memory of Her* by Elisabeth Schüssler Fiorenza, a Catholic biblical scholar prominent on the American scene.

Collaboration among Catholic biblical scholars in this country has been notable. In the past two decades several important publishing ventures have involved teams of scholars. The *Jerome Biblical Commentary*, published by Prentice-Hall in 1968, and edited by Raymond Brown, Joseph Fitzmyer and Roland Murphy was a landmark. More than a quarter of a million copies were in print by 1984. In one massive volume are provided commentaries on every book of the Bible in addition to topical articles on key issues. Over fifty Catholic biblical scholars (only two of them women and no laity—another sign of the times) collaborated in its production. Other notable collaborations were the *Old Testament Reading Guides* and the *New Testament Reading Guides* published by the Liturgical Press of Collegeville, Minnesota under the general editorship of William G. Heidt, O.S.B., Barnabas Ahern, C.P., Kathryn Sullivan, R.S.C.J. and Carroll Stuhlmueller, C.P. These remarkable booklet commentaries (31 volumes on the Old Testament and 14 on the New) remained in print for more than twenty years (first appearing in 1960). Their replacement—*The Collegeville Bible Commentary*—under the editorial direction of Robert Karris, O.F.M. and Dianne Bergant, C.S.A. have recently appeared. Other collaborative series would be that of the Paulist Press with 48 booklets edited by Neil J. McEleney, C.S.P. between 1960 and 1975 and the *New Testament Message* (edited by Wilfrid Harrington, O.P. and Donald Senior, C.P.) and the *Old Testament Message* (edited by Martin McNamara, M.S.C. and Carroll Stuhlmueller, C.P.), both published by Michael Glazier, Inc.

These and other joint projects are testimony to the substantial community of Catholic biblical scholarship in America. The purpose of each of these ventures is to bring the best of contemporary scholarship to a wide audience—a pastoral goal in direct connection with the spirit and directives of Vatican II. It would be empty chauvinism to suggest that the biblical movement has had more success or vigor in this country than it has elsewhere; no such comparison is implied here. We wish simply to note that the monumental endorsement given to the role of the Bible in Catholic thought and life by Vatican II has been implemented in the American church with astounding energy and even success.

Impact of the Biblical Renewal on Popular Piety

Two outstanding Catholic scholars struck the fire of enthusiasm in popular ranks, Fr. Bruce Vawter, C.M., and Fr. John L. McKenzie. In 1955 Vawter published *A Popular Explanation of the Four Gospels* (Our Sunday Visitor Press, 445 pages, $2.25!). Lest continuity with earlier American catechetical tradition be lost, this too belonged to the series, *Father Smith Instructs Jackson*, a classic in old style apologetics which Vawter introduced into the modern age! In the following year Vawter published *A Path Through Genesis*. Together these two books opened a new age of interpretation on the American Catholic scene. A more comprehensive presentation was undertaken by John L. McKenzie in *The Two-Edged Sword*, also in 1956. The publishers of the latter two books—Sheed & Ward and Bruce (both now defunct)—deserve a bouquet of credit for bringing the biblical movement into the rank and file of Catholic America. These important Catholic presses would be joined by Herder of St. Louis, then Herder and Herder of New York, Newman Press of Westminster, MD, Liturgical Press, Paulist Press and others already mentioned in this chapter. Significantly *The Two-Edged Sword* was held up for a considerable time by Jesuit censors, until it was released through the intervention of two leading Canadian Jesuit scholars, Fr. Roderick A.F.MacKenzie and Fr. David Stanley. Fr. Gerard S. Sloyan's review of *The Two-Edged Sword* began appropriately by extolling this "supremely important book," which offered not only clear insightful language but also unmistakable signposts for travelling into all parts of the Old Testament. In 1975, on the occasion of his sixty-fifth birthday, McKenzie was honored with a Festschrift, *No Famine in the Land*, with a full list of his publications from 1933 onward, technical and popular, with photos from the day of his first communion to his presidency of the CBA (1963-64) and of the Society of Biblical Literature (1966). Perhaps the most monumental of great books from John L. McKenzie is his *Dictionary of the Bible*, a book of 954 pages and 800,000 words which the *Journal of Biblical Literature* described as "simply amazing ... every important subject and person commonly regarded as biblical is treated, and never simply," but always in a popularly understandable style.

The auspicious start given to popular biblical materials by giants like these has continued and developed without pause. There are a number of periodicals focusing exclusively on biblical topics. The pioneer popular journal *The Bible Today* has continued since its start in 1962. It has been joined by the somewhat more technical *Biblical Theology Bulletin*, which reaches back in its origins to the Latin language magazine *Verbum Domini*, begun at the Pontifical Biblical Institute in Rome and then transferred to this country. *Share the Word* from the Paulist Office for Evangelization in Washington, DC, uses brief reflections on the lectionary readings to reach out to the unchurched. The wonderful explosion of charismatic piety in the past two decades has been nourished by such biblical publications as *God's Word Today* and *God's Word Among Us*.

To these have been joined a steady stream of series and individual publications intended to satisfying the insatiable appetite of American Catholics for biblical materials. The *Herald Biblical Booklets* and the *Read and Pray* series from the Franciscan Herald Press and a number of biblical discussion booklets from Pueblo Publishing Company would be good examples. Companies like Credence Cassettes (the NCR publishing company), Argus, Alba House, Paulist Press, Liturgical Press, St. Anthony Messenger Press head a growing list of companies presenting biblical studies on audio-cassettes, video and other media.

As American Catholicism moves through the eighties perhaps one of the most vibrant signs of its new life has been the renewed vigor of Catholic publishing. After the sharp fall-off of the late sixties and early seventies when several revered names in Catholic publishing bit the dust, new houses such as Michael Glazier, Inc., Winston, Servant, Pueblo Publications, Peter Li, Inc., and Living Flame Press have burst on the scene—all of them providing a heavy menu of popular biblical materials. Needless to say, Orbis Books, under the guidance of Philip Scharper, found its own important niche amid this wide variety of Catholic publishers.

The Ecumenical Dimension

One of the distinctive features of the American Catholic church has been its ecumenical involvement. Because of the variety of Christian denominations in this country and the pluralistic caste of our society, it is not surprising that what is often a theoretical possibility for many Catholics in Europe or Latin American is a pragmatic reality here.

This is certainly the case in the area of biblical scholarship. A common text and common methodologies have bonded Protestants and Catholics in the area of biblical research to a degree unsurpassed in any other discipline. As already noted, a vivid symbol of that reality was the election of a Protestant scholar, Paul Achtemeier, as President of the Catholic Biblical Association of America in 1983. That election was not merely a grand gesture. Achtemeier and many other Protestant scholars have been active participants in the CBA for years. And the same is true for the Society of Biblical Literature, a national professional organization that was for many years predominantly Protestant in membership and ethos. As already mentioned, John L. McKenzie was its first Catholic president and George MacRae, S.J. was its executive director from 1973 to 1976. Hundreds of Catholic scholars participate in the Society and attend its annual meetings.

Such pragmatic ecumenical contacts extend across every phase of biblical scholarship. A Catholic student in exegesis routinely uses Protestant scholarship and Protestants use Catholic. At most major graduate schools of biblical studies, the percentages of Catholics and Protestants will reflect national demographics rather than ideological bias. Major commentary series such as *The Anchor Bible* (Doubleday) or *Hermeneia* (Fortress Press) draw on Catholic and Protestant scholarship without even needing to declare they are "ecumenical." And it has been the biblical movement that produced a phenomenon perhaps unprecedented in Christian scholarship in the past 500 years: two works on ecumenically sensitive topics that not only involved collaboration between Protestants and Catholics but managed to produce a single consensus text on such issues. The two books, *Peter in the New Testament* (Paulist, 1973) and *Mary in the New Testament* (Paulist, 1978) originated in the United States Lutheran-Roman Catholic bilateral dialogues and were expanded to include scholars from several major denominations.

Where deep divisions exist in the realm of biblical studies, it is less across denominational lines than it is between those who accept the historical critical methodologies and those who consider it inappropriate for the Bible.

The resurgence of the Bible in Catholic liturgical life and piety, as discussed above, has also had a genuine, if more subtle, impact on how Catholics in general view Protestants in this country. For many American Catholics Bible study or Bible prayer groups had once been tagged "Protestant" — and therefore something no self-respecting Catholic would be caught doing. But with such experiences not only tolerated but encouraged, not a few Catholics have become aware that things could be learned from the Protestant churches and that Catholicism's claim on the one true faith could be made too exclusive.

Problems and Issues Remaining

If there remain some outstanding questions still to be addressed to the Bible, we should not be surprised but rather rejoice in the fact. When the Jewish people complete the yearly cycle of reading the Torah, or the five books of Moses, they never stop with the final verse of the last chapter of Deuteronomy, the fifth book of Moses, but instead they begin without interruption to read from chapter one of Genesis. This conclusion and new beginning occurs on the final day of the feast of Tabernacles, called *simhat ha-torah*, meaning "the joy of the Torah." We are reminded of the statement of Pope Pius XII in his encyclical on biblical studies, *Divino Afflante Spiritu*:

> Moreover we may rightly and deservedly hope that our times also can contribute something towards the deeper and more accurate interpretation of Sacred Scripture. For not a few things, especially in matters of history, were scarcely at all or not fully explained by the commentators of past ages, since they lacked almost all the information, which was needed for their clearer exposition... A more profound knowledge of antiquity has given rise to new questions ....Quite wrongly therefore do some pretend. . .that nothing remains to be added by the Catholic exegete of our time. . . .These our times have brought to light so many things which call for a fresh investigation and a new examination (n. 31-32).
> . . .no one will be surprised if all difficulties are not yet solved and overcome; but that even today serious problems greatly exercise the minds of Catholic exegetes (n. 44).

Questions do remain: peace within our nuclear age and its terrifying danger of nuclear holocaust; economics and the plight of the poor; dispossessed families within the inner city and across the farmbelt; the active role of the laity within the church, laity far more educated theologically than at any previous age of the church, for that matter in any century of biblical history; the recognition of the rights of minorities within our culture and our church, so that in the USA our church leadership and our worship visibly and symbolically represent who we are as the people of God, women as well as men, black, red and yellow as well as the color white, Hispanic and oriental as well as anglo.

To transmit into specific terms for today the phrase of Pope Pius XII, "difficulties. . .not yet solved and overcome," we need to continue searching the Scriptures about the ministerial role of women, a task already initiated by the Pontifical Biblical Commission in Rome and the CBA of America. There is also the continuous task of translating the Bible so that its message of justice and liberation, its call for holiness and apostolate are rightly heard, so that no one be excluded. Foremost in this task is the need of an *Inclusive Language Lectionary*; the one published by the National Council of Churches of Christ in the USA (October 1983) needs further refinement.

Still more pressing is the gigantic undertaking of translating the Bible into the more than three thousand languages (many of them without a written form) still without the Bible. The Catholic couple, Paul and Ginny Witte, founders of LOGOS Translators, are setting their hands firmly to ploughing this virginal field.

Fear is being voiced by some that "tradition" is being reversed and denied by the post-Conciliar church of the eighties. A new wave of "fundamentalism" seems to sweeping our country and church. This kind of fundamentalism can become very negative as it denies any development in our understanding of the Bible and Catholic doctrine. Questions like slavery and health care were never adequately solved even in New Testament documents. Other specifically American questions like separation of church and state and freedom of conscience face us today in ways never clearly anticipated in biblical times where union of church and state was simply taken for granted. False fundamentalism is generally shortsighted and equates tradition with the past hundred years or anachronistically the thirteenth century as the greatest of them all.

True "fundamentalism," on the other hand, reaches into the most basic or fundamental issues of today (food, hunger, war, oppression) and addresses these questions with the full scope of the church's tradition, including its powerful roots in the biblical witness of the Old and New Testaments.

Philip Scharper was a truly Catholic "fundamentalist" in the best biblical sense of the term. In his direction of Orbis Books, he exemplified the history of the Catholic biblical movement in the USA. The pastoral origins of the CBA mirrored his determination to tackle the serious world problems of war, hunger, and social, sexual and racial injustices of our day. The pain, conflict the suspicion at times directed to the Catholic biblical movement have cut their own lines deep into the heart of this gentle man at Orbis Books. The determination to remain a Catholic publisher associated with the Catholic foreign mission society of Maryknoll, along with the courage to look outward upon the world as a missionary must, finds its parallel in the development of the Catholic biblical movement. At first, it was a group of one hundred clerics ordained within the Roman Catholic church, but by 1984 it included over 800 members, men and women, ordained and lay, Protestant and Jewish as well as Catholic. The goal of the association remained the same, to "devote itself to the scientific study of the Bible .... in conformity with the spirit and the instructions of the Catholic church," yet the realization grew that this goal could best be achieved in collaboration with those outside the boundaries of Catholicism.

While the biblical movement rests squarely upon the results of scientific study, it is not confined to scholarship. Its most flourishing expression is to be seen in Bible study groups and workshops across the country, in the wide variety of pastoral publications, books and magazines, cassettes and audio-visual aids, in updated and effective preaching of the Word.

We are, therefore, proud to honor the inspiring person of Philip Scharper and his wife and co-worker, Sally Scharper.

American Catholic Theology Now

∽ ✻ ↶

Monika K. Hellwig

Our predecessors would certainly find us shocking. Our contemporaries in other lands and other faiths find us interesting, often puzzling, sometimes annoying. But our successors may find us rather more entertaining than otherwise, and perhaps even quite instructive. We are the generation of American Catholic theologians to whom too much has happened too quickly. Indeed, we have been visited with the Chinese curse, "may you live in interesting times."

Heirs of the struggle over Americanism that left the lately immigrant local church somewhat Rome-bound and unsure of itself, we have nevertheless come into the intoxicating freedom of Vatican II and its aftermath. It has left us experimenting with our freedom, sometimes cautiously enough but in some cases rather like adolescents — exhibiting just as much energy, enthusiasm and restlessness, and not knowing without practical experi-

ment how far our self-assertion might be able to go.
Caught between the expectations of American democratic process and academic freedom on the one hand and
severely centralized and autocratic Roman *magisterium* on
the other hand, our theology has necessarily been
entangled with issues of Canon Law, questions of authority, and disputes over censorship. We have been accustomed to keeping our eyes and ears trained respectfully
upon Europe and its great universities in the past, but we
are now being overtaken by newly insistent and persuasive voices from the Southern hemisphere and from
among the poor and dispossessed of the earth. Moreover,
among ourselves there are fewer Roman collars, both
because of the infiltration of laity female and male into the
ranks, and also because ordained professors at universities
and colleges have come to define their theologizing rather
more firmly in an academic than in a clerical context.

This, then, is the situation in which we have shaped and
are shaping the process and products of American
Catholic theology in the 1980s. The most obvious feature
of that theology is that we are writing and publishing in
unprecedented volume, scope and boldness. Moreover,
publishers have been giving us so much encouragement in
this, that we can conclude that we are being read rather
widely — sometimes even in translation. This last has
come as something of a surprise, for there had been a tacit
assumption that translation went in the other direction:
"real theology" was produced in Europe, and we
expected our publishers and their talent scouts to pick up
seminal books across the Atlantic and have them translated and relayed to us as rapidly as possible, so that we
could "keep up." We looked to journals such as *Theology
Digest* and *Concilium* to keep us informed of what was

happening in the theological "heartland." I believe most
of us are still rather astonished when we find issues of
Concilium edited by some of our own, and relaying American thought to Europe and elsewhere. And it is with
similar surprise that we begin to realize that some of the
best contemporary scholarship and some of the most creative synthetic thought is coming out of our own great
universities on this side of the Atlantic.

In the midst of such a period of new awakening and
many-faceted theological activity, both in live exchanges
and in publications, it would not be possible to offer an
exhaustive list of North American initiatives and accomplishments in the various disciplines of theological endeavor. But it will be of interest to look at some
representative and characteristic sections of these. Fundamental theology, for instance, has truly begun to flourish
among North American Catholic theologians. Many if
not most who are in this field are constantly involved in
scholarly exchanges across denominational boundaries,
and in a continuing dialogue with colleagues on philosophical faculties. As a result, fundamental theology has
come much further into the public forum of the intellectual life of our own times, paying close attention to the
critique of theory that has taken place in relation to the
natural sciences, to new philosophical reflection on the
nature of our approach to truth and to reality in human
thought, and to the historical perspectives that shed light
on traditional formulations and interpretations. Because
of the pervasive contemporary North American experience of religious and cultural plurality, there is a heightened awareness of cultural relativity, which necessarily
influences the way we search for the foundations of our
theological convictions and formulations. Frequently,

therefore, we are in quest not so much of credibility as of intelligibility for theological discourse and theological positions.[1] As might be expected, this is accompanied by a renewed interest in questions of theological method.[2]

On a more popular level there is a new direction and style in what might nevertheless still be called apologetics. The new apologetics goes arm in arm with ecumenism. That is to say that it has left behind triumphalist claims on behalf of the institutional Catholic Church, but it has also passed on beyond self-denigrating embarrassment over the characteristics of Catholicism, and has come to a certain comfortable appreciation of complementarity. This is very evident in the work of the various bi-lateral ecumenical consultations, both at the national and at the local and regional levels. It is also evident in recent Catholic publications for the educated general reader.[3]

In the content of systematic theology there continue to be attempts, as there always will be and must be, to fashion a synthesis of the whole belief system which will render it most intelligible to contemporary believers and seekers. Attempts to do this in terms of existential and

[1]Outstanding examples of the contemporary Catholic American interest in fundamental theology are: David Tracy, *Blessed Rage for Order: the New Pluralism in Theology* (NY: Seabury, 1975), and *The Analogical Imagination: Christian Theology and the Culture of Pluralism* (NY: Crossroad, 1981); and Francis Schussler Fiorenza, *Foundational Theology: Jesus and the Church* (NY: Crossroad, 1984).

[2]A good idea of the extent of American Catholic interest in method in theology is to be had from J.J. Mueller's *What Are they Saying about Theological Method?* (NY: Paulist, 1984).

[3]Though not exactly from an American author, Rosemary Haughton's *The Catholic Thing* (Springfield: Templegate, 1979), and *The Passionate God* (NY: Paulist, 1981), provide striking examples of this. The same stance of accepted complementarity is intended in Monika Hellwig, *Understanding Catholicism* (NY: Paulist, 1981).

phenomenological analysis of experience are certainly still alive, but seem no longer to hold the center of the stage. Likewise, the effects of process thought continue to be felt in theological reflection and debate, but rather more diffusely than in earlier decades.[4] What has truly come to the fore are the demands of the socio-critical perspectives in philosophy, theology and the human sciences, and among these more particularly those of the liberation theories of Latin America and the Third World. Although North American theologians have been, on the whole, strangely reluctant to acknowledge the urgency and force of the questions being raised from this quarter, the solid, decades-long effort of Philip Scharper and Orbis Books is beginning in the eighties to yield some results in a more general North American response. It was Scharper's truly prophetic discernment and commitment that brought us a steady stream of translations of the vanguard and seminal publications of Latin American liberation theology while other publishing houses continued to look almost exclusively to Europe for significant texts to translate. Moreover, it was with the encouragement and support of Orbis Books under Philip Scharper's leadership, that the process and the book entitled *Theology in the Americas* came into existence, drawing large numbers of North American theologians and church people into the dialogue with "liberation theology" which they had tried to avoid.[5]

---

[4]*Cf.* the reflections on where the matter of process theology now stands by Bernard Lee, "The Two Process Theologies," *Theological Studies* 45 (1984), no. 2, and Joseph A. Bracken, "The Two Process Theologies: a Reappraisal," *Theological Studies* 46 (1985), no. 1.

[5]Philip Scharper and Orbis Books introduced to North Americans Gustavo Gutierrez, Juan Luis Segundo, Ignacio Ellacuria, Hugo Assmann, Jon Sobrino, and a host of others. The extent to which these authors have become partners in dialogue with U.S. Catholic theologians is witnessed among other

It is perhaps the insistent presence of the voices of the Third World liberation theologians among us that is responsible in large part for the shift in focus of systematic theology among Catholic theologians of North America. There appears to have been a swing from preoccupation with creation and Christian anthropology in the sixties, through a concentration on eschatology in the seventies, over to a deepening, steadying concern with Christology and soteriology in the eighties. After decades of silence on Christology, the time seems all at once to be ripe for new reflection, for there has been a veritable explosion of new attempts to render traditional Catholic Christology intelligible in the terms in which we today think and perceive.[6] What all these contributions reveal, however, is that there is still a great need to move our systematic theology into the arena of the wider ecumenism, bringing our understanding of Jesus Christ and of the process of salvation into dialogue with visions and hopes of salvation presented by traditions such as the Buddhist and the Marxist. We seem to be at the very beginning of such ventures, but the great American conspiracy to ignore Marxism and hope it will go away, appears at long last to

things by the pattern and content of the Woodstock Theological Center publications and conferences, the recurrence of their themes and ideas at the the annual conferences of the Catholic Theological Society of America, and by the frequency of courses and lectures on liberation theology in Catholic universities, colleges and seminaries of North America.

[6]*E.g.* Frans Jozef van Beeck, *Christ Proclaimed: Christology as Rhetoric* (NY: Paulist, 1979); James Patrick Mackey, *Jesus, the Man and the Myth: Contemporary Christology* (NY: Paulist, 1979); Michael L. Cook, *The Jesus of Faith* (NY: Paulist, 1981); John Pawlikowski, *Christ in the Light of the Jewish-Christian Dialogue* (NY: Paulist, 1982); Monika K. Hellwig, *Jesus the Compassion of God* (Wilmington: Michael Glazier, 1983), to mention only a few, without any reference to those studies of Christology that are primarily biblical or historical.

be breaking down, at least among the theologians.[7]

It is not only the impact of Third World theology that has drawn North American Catholic theology into the realm of public issues. There has also emerged a lively inter-action between the positions and statements of the U.S. Conference of Catholic Bishops and the activities and preoccupations of the Catholic theologians. While this has, of course, been most marked in moral and pastoral theology, it is not absent from the realms of systematic theology. These exchanges have been occasioned by episcopal statements on race relations, poverty, armaments and the functioning of the U.S. economy. In such exchange it is possible under present circumstances to have very fruitful and amicable cooperation between the hierarchy and theologians. There are, however, other questions, which render the collaboration far more delicate and difficult. In matters concerning sexual and family morality, political roles filled by vowed religious, the position of women in Christian community and worship, and some similarly critical issues, tension and conflict between theologians and hierarchy are predictable and inevitable. The tension between the need for creative thought and problem-solving in the local situation and in the ecumenical context on the one hand, and centralized Roman teaching so resistant to change and so impervious to testimony from the grassroots of Christian experience on the other hand, puts the U.S. Bishops in an entirely unenviable position.

This paradox of unprecedented collaboration at a time of sharply increasing tensions is resulting in some groundbreaking new reflection on the nature of authority in the

---

[7]Noteworthy among existing published studies is Arthur F. McGovern, *Marxism: an American Christian Perspective* (NY: Orbis, 1981).

Church, and on the complementarity of the different types of authority represented by the office-holders and by those with scholarly and practical expertise.[8] This effort in systematic theology has been met in a very helpful way by the work and interest of the Canon Law Society of America.[9] Yet the tension is inescapable and is kept constantly before the public eye by the continuing lack of due process as we of the Anglo-Saxon tradition understand that term. What is evident to common sense and critical reflection about the ways in which truth can and cannot be ascertained is frequently denied on authoritarian grounds which are increasingly difficult to defend in the light of history. And so the issue of the appropriate complementarity of authority is kept alive and seems to present a peculiarly appropriate task to American Catholic theologians in the 1980s.

Meanwhile, institutional and political aspects of theology have not prevented sacramental theology from reasserting itself. The long preparation of the fifties, sixties and seventies is beginning to fructify in this area. The painstaking work of the Collegeville Benedictines in the history and phenomenology of liturgy, in patristic theology, textual studies and pastoral reflection has prepared the ground. So also has the cross-fertilizing effort of the

[8]This includes notably: Avery Dulles, *A Church to Believe in: Discipleship and the Dynamics of Freedom* (NY: Crossroad, 1982), pursuing further the theme opened up in Part II of *The Survival of Dogma* (NY: Doubleday, 1971), a theme that Dulles has also discussed in *Chicago Studies*, no. 17 (summer 1978) and in the *Proceedings of the Catholic Theological Society of America*. no. 35, (1980); and Francis A. Sullivan *Magisterium* (NY: Paulist, 1983).

[9]As witnessed eloquently in Leo J. O'Donovan, ed., *Cooperation between Theologians and the Ecclesiastical Magisterium*, a *Report of the Joint Committee of the Canon Law Society of America and the Catholic Theological Society of America* (Washington: Catholic University of America, 1982).

Notre Dame summer school of liturgy, which since the 1950s introduced a steady stream of great European liturgical, biblical and patristic scholars to the North American scene through their personal presence in summer sessions and through the publication of the lectures that were given. Now that the changes of the Second Vatican Council have been largely assimilated into our liturgical celebration and the scholarly understanding of what lay behind them has been more widely assimilated, there has been a veritable explosion of new publications in the area of sacramental theology.[10]

What seems to be at stake is the reappropriation of the sacramental principle at a time when secularization appears to have run its course and spent itself upon the sands of time. The concern is not to defend Catholic doctrinal formulation against those of the Protestant traditions, nor to try to establish the institution of seven particular sacraments by Jesus in person, but to rediscover the sacramentality by which faith is expressed and nurtured in all aspects of Christian life and to relate the high ecclesiastical celebrations which we have traditionally dignified with the capital S to that more pervasive working of the sacramental principle in daily life.[11] The enterprise, therefore, is now both historical and constructive, involving perspectives both from the social sciences and from the history of religions, and exploring psychological insights into the uses and effects of ritual. The more

[10]Besides the continuing series of publications from Collegeville Liturgical Press, and various significant contributions to sacramental theology from Orbis and from Paulist Press, there are for instance the completed series, *The Message of the Sacraments* from Michael Glazier, Inc., and the series in sacramental theology still in production from Pueblo Press.

[11]This is a perspective developed explicitly by Bernard Cooke, *Sacraments and Sacramentality* (Mystic, CT: XXIII Press, 1983).

ecumenical approach to sacramental theology has meant a
link with questions of peace and social justice and has
tended towards a focus on the finality of the sacraments in
order to discover in that focus the possibilities of growth
and adaptation. These two trends have become clearly
evident in the concerns addressed by the Liturgical Conference, the Canadian Liturgical Society and the Collegeville Ecumenical Center in the last few years.

Much of this growth and development may be attributed to an increasing interest in the history of theology
and spirituality. Although still relatively poorly represented in courses offered in graduate and undergraduate
theology programs, historical theological studies are
richly endowed by current publications.[12] On the assumption that publishing houses do not intend to court bank-
ruptcy, the sheer volume of primary sources being
published in new editions and new translations suggests
widening circles of voracious readers of historical texts.
This seems to me to indicate a certain maturity of theological interest and awareness. More particularly, it seems to
indicate a willingness to quarry the rich sources of our
tradition in order to answer the questions of our own
times constructively. This is a great advance on the colonial consciousness dominant quite recently, by which we
looked to contemporary European theology for ready-
made answers to our questions. So far, the return to the
sources appears to be particularly strong in relation to the
writers of the patristic period, and writers of the great

[12]There are, for instance, besides the continuing *Ancient Christian Writers*
series, the Michael Glazier series *The Message of the Fathers*, anthologies
of the Fathers on various topics of current interest, the Paulist *Christian
Classics* series and *Classics of Christian Spirituality* series, not to mention
the new interest evinced by serveal presses which are not primarily Catholic in reviving primary sources.

spirituality traditions. But the time may already be coming in which we make our peace again on new terms with our mediaeval theological heritage, and even (who knows?) with the theological struggles of the post-Tridentine Church now seen in the light of primary sources that yield an understanding of where we have been and where we are.[13]

In any case, the increasing historical awareness among American Catholic theologians has been fostered by widely dispersed, healthy ecumenical exchanges, and has in turn enriched these exchanges, and it is clear that there will not soon be a road back into the theological ghetto with its sheltering of the intellectually weak and its systematic deprivation of the intellectually enterprising. There is a certain heady freedom in the established fact that almost all courses, conferences, publications and other exchanges are now inevitably in some measure ecumenical and are therefore subjected to scholarly criteria of a wider forum than the intra-denominational ecclesiastical one. This offers the American Catholic theologians of our time a new kind of personal freedom and a new kind of personal responsibility. As a matter of personal professional survival in the academic "marketplace," scholarly competence rather than denominational orthodoxy is the primary criterion for employment in academic institutions. Even where hierarchic censorship intervenes in a particular institution, there is a world of other employment opportunities beyond hierarchic control. This kind of freedom gives rise to an entirely new kind of responsibility for theologians — a responsibility to the tradition

---

[13]The work in which Carl Peter has been engaged for some decades at the Catholic University of America, seems to be a happy indication of the way this might happen.

and its wisdom that is wider than any institutional censorship can claim, and far more subtle than any censor could
require. And this becomes a corporate responsibility for
continuing discussion and discernment which gives a more
central role to professional associations with an explicit
denominational reference, such as the Catholic Theological Society of America.

All that has been written here so far has perhaps given
all too placid and one-dimensional a sense of what is
happening in North America Catholic theology. It has
not, for instance, adverted to the great concerns over the
question of women's participation in the process of
Church decision-making and the challenge that presents
to the traditional Catholic ecclesiology which has been
constructed around institutional experiences and presup-
positions which appear to our contemporary eyes to be in
contradiction of reality. That concern, in turn, leads to
the question of the role that women ought to play in the
theology itself, where a certain left-wing contingent
would call for a radical subversion of the theological
process as we know it, while others call simply for continuing participation, expecting that it will lead to some as
yet undetermined modifications, without any need for
aggressive caucussing activities. Something similar may
be said of the Hispanic voices in the North American
Church, which are only now becoming sufficiently
numerous and established and sophisticated to raise questions concerning their characteristic and complementary
role in North American Catholic theological reflection.
Even more pertinently and interestingly, there is the
question of black Catholic voices in the theological discourse, coming as they frequently do from a different
church experience in which the denominational and eth-

nic elements were blended, and finding in Catholicism a certain cultural alienation to be overcome.

The tasks ahead for the Catholic theological community of North America seem to include the integration of many extremely urgent and politically sensitive issues such as peace and non-violence, poverty and social justice, ecology and racial harmony, respect for human life and bio-ethical issues, into a viable and synthetic interpretation of the faith in our own context. However, these tasks also include the effective, high-level popularization of an interpretation of the faith by which American Catholics can really live in all the challenges and demands of our society. What we have at present is a dangerous trend to flee into a new and thoroughly unviable fundamentalism on the part of Catholics who are not being helped to find the answers to new questions in any way which they can recognize as giving them continuity with the faith of their forebears. The responsibility which this confers on the American Catholic theologians of our time is something more demanding and more heavily consequential than the former kind of institutional answerability for orthodoxy. But as long as we call ourselves Catholic there is no doubt that we also face the task of maintaining the unity of the universal Church while dealing honestly with our particular questions. We are indeed visited with the Chinese curse: we live in interesting times.

Liberation Theology
and the
World Church

❦

John Eagleson

If we are to understand American Catholicism in the 1980s, we need to look not only to ourselves, but beyond ourselves. "Yo soy yo y mis circunstancias," said Spanish philosopher Jose Ortega y Gasset. "I am I and my circumstances," I am I and all that is around me. And today more than ever our circumstances embrace the planet.

I cite here examples from the churches around the world that I think are emblematic of the "circumstances" in which we find ourselves.

- In a village in West Africa a Catholic priest is initiated into a confraternity of healers, of witchdoctors, culminating his own spiritual odyssey and his struggle to correlate the healing power of Jesus with traditional healing rites.
- In Sri Lanka a Christian lives for two years in a Buddhist monastery, studying the sacred Buddhist

texts, rethinking his Christian identity in Buddhist categories.

- At Union Theological Seminary in New York, one of the foremost black theologians in the U.S. finds his thinking profoundly influenced by his experience among the Minjung theologians of Korea.

- In Nicaragua, near the Honduran border, a small Christian community of poor campesinos, a *comunidad de base*, gathers to read the Bible together and to discuss what it means to turn the other cheek to the band of U.S.-supported *contras* that just burned down their clinic and kidnapped four young people from their village.

- Brazilian Franciscan theologian Leonardo Boff is called to Rome to defend his views before the Vatican Congregation for the Doctrine of the Faith. His writings, in which he criticizes the arbitrary use of centralized power in the Church, are described as "dangerous." Although Boff agrees to comply with Vatican directives, he nonetheless is later ordered to enter into an indefinite period of "penitential silence."

Not all of these images have to do with liberation theology, but they all have to do with a momentous shift in the Church. To understand liberation theology — as well as our situation as American Catholics in the 1980s — it is helpful to know something about this shift in the Church and in theology.

The Coming of the World Church

The West African priest, the Sri Lankan in a Buddhist monastery, the Minjung theologians, the Nicaraguan *comunidades de base*, Leonardo Boff — all are from what we have traditionally called "mission lands." These are the churches of the periphery, churches often established by and frequently dependent on the so-called sending churches of the Euro-American centers.

This model, however, of an ecclesiastical center and its dependent periphery, of sending churches and mission churches, has become not only inadequate but obsolete.

To cite the case of the Catholic Church, in 1900 77 percent of the Catholic population was found in the North Atlantic nations and 23 percent in the Third World. Projections for the year 2000 indicate that approximately 30 percent of the Catholic Church membership will be found in Northern nations, while 70 percent will be found in the Third World.

Such changes have not gone unnoticed by astute commentators on the Church. Swiss missiologist Walbert Buhlmann calls this phenomenon "the coming of the Third Church." Harvey Cox points to the significance of this church of the poor and holds up Nicaraguan Ernesto Cardenal and the *comunidades de base* as signs of hope and portents of the Church of the future.

German theologian Karl Rahner refers to the end of Euro-American dominated Christianity as the coming of "the World Church." The significance he ascribes to this phenomenon is demonstrated by his division of all of Church history into three epochs: The first epoch was the short period of Jewish Christianity during which the Gospel was proclaimed in Israel and to it. The second epoch was that of Gentile Christianity, when the Gospel was preached and churches established within the relatively homogeneous Hellenistic-European cultural world. The second epoch lasted from the first century into the twentieth century. The third epoch is that of world

Christianity, which Rahner dates, very roughly, from the time of the Second Vatican Council (see "Towards a Fundamental Theological Interpretation of Vatican II," in *Theological Studies*, December 1979, pp. 716-26).

It is only recently, in the last twenty years or so, that the churches outside the North Atlantic center have begun in a significant way to articulate their faith in their own terms, to speak from their own faith experience. Up until the time of the Vatican Council, according to Rahner, "the actual concrete activity of the Church in its relation to the world outside of Europe was in fact (if you will pardon the expression) the activity of an export firm which exported a European religion as a commodity it did not really want to change but sent throughout the world together with the rest of the culture and civilization it considered superior" (ibid., p. 717). The European nations had their colonies and the European churches had their missions. All this has begun to change in the years following Vatican Council II.

Since the 1960s the churches of Asia, of Africa, and of Latin America have begun to speak from their own experience. No longer do they always look to the sending churches before they speak. Their theology and religious reflection is no longer derivative. In the words of Peruvian liberation theologian Gustavo Gutierrez, "they drink from their own wells."

And when the churches outside the North Atlantic countries began to speak for themselves, one of the things they spoke about was liberation and one of the ways they spoke it was liberation theology.

Liberation Theology

What exactly is liberation theology, and where did it come from?

Liberation theologians count themselves as part of a long and rich heritage. Among the first liberation theologians were those Old Testament writers who told the story of the Exodus, the liberation of the Hebrews from the harsh oppression in Egypt.

Although the Latin American Church has often been in league with the Pharaohs of the continent, there has always been a strong liberation tradition as well. For example, the Dominican friar Bartolome de las Casas (1474-1566) is affectionately remembered as the "Defender of the Indians" for his courageous protests before the Spanish crown against cruel exploitation by gold-hungry conquistadors.

Modern-day liberation theology takes its inspiration not only from a long history of a downtrodden people's struggle for justice, but also from the great social encyclicals: *Rerum Novarum* (Pope Leo XIII), *Quadragesimo Anno* (Pius XI), *Mater et Magistra* (John XXIII), and *Populorum Progressio* (Paul VI).

Vatican Council II, in its Pastoral Constitution on the Church in the Modern World, likewise expressed the Church's commitment to the poor, proclaiming that "the joys and the hopes, the griefs and the anxieties of the people of this age, especially those who are poor or in any way afflicted, these too are the joys, and hopes, the griefs and anxieties of the followers of Christ" (no. 1).

The Church's social teaching passed a milestone when the Second Synod of Bishops declared in 1971 that the Gospel supports "action on behalf of justice and participation in the transformation of the world" as "a constitutive dimension of the Church's mission for the redemption of the human race and its liberation from every oppressive situation" (*Justice in the World*, no. 6).

Eight years later the Latin American bishops declared at their conference in Puebla, Mexico, that, "we affirm the need for conversion on the part of the whole Church to a preferential option for the poor, an option aimed at their integral liberation" (no. 1134).

When theologians in Latin America began to apply the social teachings of the Church to the wretched conditions of Latin America, modern-day Latin American liberation theology was born. One of these theologians is Gustavo Gutierrez, whose experience in many ways is typical of the Latin American liberation theologians and encapsulates the beginnings of liberation theology. Like many of the most promising seminarians of his day, Gutierrez was sent to Europe to study; he was exposed to the progressive European theology that helped prepare the ground for Vatican Council II. But when Gutierrez returned home to Lima he found that the application of his European theology was not a simple task. Gutierrez speaks of what he discovered on returning to Lima:

> I discovered three things. I discovered that *poverty was destructive*, something to be fought against and destroyed, not merely something that was the object of our charity. Second, I discovered that *poverty was not accidental*. The fact that these people are poor and not rich is not just a matter of chance, but the result of a structure. . . . Third, I discovered that *poor people were a social class*. When I discovered that poverty was something to be fought against, that poverty was structural, that poor people were a class and could organize, it became crystal clear that in order to serve the poor, one had to move into political action (Robert McAfee Brown, *Gustavo Gutierrez*, John Knox Press, 1980, p. 23).

Gutierrez's homecoming from France to Peru represented his own passing over from Rahner's second epoch of European Christianity to the third epoch of World Christianity.

In catechism class in elementary school I remember the nun giving us the following case: "Mr. Jones is very poor. One morning he was walking down the street and he spotted a bottle of milk on the doorstep of the Smith family, who was very rich (In those days milk was delivered to doorsteps). If Mr. Jones takes that milk bottle home to his hungry children, is he committing a sin?" We dutifully answered that he was not.

Indeed, Thomas Aquinas whose name became synonymous with traditional Roman Catholic theology, taught in his *Summa Theologiae* that "in extreme necessity all goods are common, that is, all goods are to be shared" (II-II q. 66, a. 7).

And Vatican Council II had said that "the right to have a share of earthly good sufficient for oneself and one's family belongs to everyone.... Persons in extreme necessity have the right to take from the riches of others what they need" (*Gaudium et Spes*, no. 69).

If the poor Mr. Jones is a rare exception in town, this traditional teaching does not present serious challenges to law and order. But what happens when nine out of ten families in town are in the same straits as Mr. Jones? What do the "milk bottle theologians" say to Mr. Jones then, and what do they say to the rich Smith family?

It was questions like these that Gutierrez had to face when he returned from France to Peru, and he faced them from and in the context of a slum in Lima, from within a community of the poor.

Gutierrez helped to establish the primary "theological place" of liberation theology (the *locus theologicus* as the professionals call it) as the struggle of ordinary people to achieve "liberty and justice for all."

Liberation theologians are unanimous in grounding their theology in the struggle of the poor, and without exception they are linked to a *comunidad de base*, one of the grassroots Christian communities springing up all over Latin America. It is the experience of these small faith communities that provides the "raw material" for theological reflection. Thus Gutierrez refers to theology as a "secondary" act; it is the people's faith experience that is primary.

"All liberation theology," adds Gutierrez, "originates among the world's anonymous, no matter who writes the books or the declarations articulating it."

Liberation theology is not just another subdivision in the theological enterprise — like moral theology or systematic theology, for example. Rather, liberation theology takes a new approach to all the great theological themes — creation, incarnation, sin, grace, salvation, redemption. It considers them from the vantage point of the poor, from the underside of history. Liberation theology is a reflection — in the light of the word of God — on the experience of poor Christians in the liberation struggles.

Liberation theology is not limited to Latin America. Indigenous versions of liberation theology have appeared in South Africa and in India, in South Korea and the Philippines, in Sri Lanka and Jamaica. Indeed it can be found anywhere people struggle to be free and try to understand their struggle in the light of the word of God.

When liberation theology first appeared on the theological scene in the late 1960s and early 1970s, there were many who dismissed it as just another theological fad, a short-lived comet that would soon fade from the theological sky.

But liberation theology has not gone away. Protestant theologian John Cobb says that "the greatest event in twentieth-century Church history was the Second Vatican Council. The greatest achievement which this event has made possible is the liberation theology and praxis of Latin America." Catholic theologian David Tracy agrees, saying, "It is now clear that the major breakthrough in Christian theology in the last decade has been the explosive emergence of political and liberation theologians." Even *Time* magazine listed Gutierrez's *A Theology of Liberation* as one of the 12 books of the 1970s that "most deserve to survive."

Liberation theology will never go away or disappear. As old as Exodus, it is as perduring as people's struggle for freedom.

The Vatican Controversy

Liberation theology has been in the headlines, particularly with the silencing of Brazilian liberation theologian Leonardo Boff.

The controversy over liberation theology can best be appreciated, I think, if we recall Rahner's three epochs. With the coming of the World Church, Christianity is moving inevitably toward pluriformity, and theological discourse is becoming multicentric. The present pope and, especially the Vatican curia, see this as a threat to Catholic uniformity and Roman unicentricity. The theological initiatives of Boff are seen as "dangerous"; the pope warns against "centrifugal forces that threaten the unity of the Church."

In September 1984, the Vatican Congregation for the Doctrine of the Faith published a document entitled

"Instruction on Certain Aspects of the 'Theology of Liberation.' "

Although it recognized that "the powerful and almost irresistible aspiration that people have for liberation constitutes one of the principal signs of the times which the Church has to interpret in the light of the Gospel" (I, 1), it also warned against "developments of that current of thought which, under the name 'theology of liberation,' proposes a novel interpretation of both the content of faith and of Christian existence which seriously departs from the faith of the Church and, in fact, actually constitutes a practical negation" (VI, 9).

But it is not so much the novel and dangerous content of liberation theology that is the Vatican concern. It is rather the locus of theological authority that worries them. The Vatican is very nervous about Christians around the world drinking from their own wells, and so the document warns that the encounter between liberation theology and the liberation experiences of the people "can be understood only in light of the specific message of revelation, authentically interpreted by the magisterium of the Church" (III, 4).

This is a classic instance of the Church of Rahner's old second epoch in confrontation with the Church of the new third epoch. The guardians of the doctrine of the faith of Euro-American Christianity are disquieted with the theologies being elaborated by theologians of the new World Church.

Boff himself criticized the perspective of the Ratzinger document: "The Instruction doesn't represent the Latin American perspective, but the European one... This is the Third World seen from a palace window."

Rahner had already posed the rhetorical question: "Do not the Roman congregations still have the mentality of a centralized bureaucracy which thinks it knows best what serves the kingdom of God and the salvation of souls throughout the world, and in such decisions takes the mentality of Rome or Italy in a frighteningly naive way as a self-evident standard?" (op. cit., pp. 717-18).

Notwithstanding Vatican intentions to the contrary, the initiative has begun to pass from Europe to the Third World, from the second epoch to the third epoch. "Rome may be the bureaucratic center of the Church," says Boff, "but it is no longer the vital mystical center."

The vital mystical center has passed from Rome to Sao Paulo, and the Vatican, which is the Holy See of the Church of the second epoch, is not letting go gracefully.

The Priest in America Today

A Reflection on Priestly Identity

❧ ❦ ❧

Robert P. Imbelli

> Great good, therefore, of such a revolution that alters not
> by exclusion, but by an enlargement...that includes the
> former, though it places it in a new point of view.
>
> (Coleridge)[1]

I — The Present Context

The reflections which follow are personal and theological in nature. They do not pretend to derive from sociological surveys, nor to proffer the "only possible" view
and approach. They proceed, rather, from one priest's,
perhaps not untypical, experience; and they offer one

[1] Samuel Taylor Coleridge, *The Notebooks*. Cited in John Coulson, *Religion and Imagination* (Oxford: Clarendon Press, 1981), p. 137.

distinctive angle of vision upon the plight and the promise of the ordained priesthood in American Catholic life today. I hope that what I have experienced and sought to express, others may find consonant with their own experience and helpful towards its clarification; and that they, in turn, may complement and complete the perspective and direction I outline here.

I should like to begin, then, on a personal note. This year marks the twentieth anniversary of my ordination to the priesthood of Jesus Christ in the Catholic Church. Twenty years in the life of any individual will be filled with seasons of joy and hope, of sadness and pain; this is but the common stuff of history and of human lives. But there can also be no denying that the past twenty years have been a time of uncommon turbulence both in Church and in nation. Many of the supposed pillars supporting both appear to have buckled. With familiar and taken-for-granted points of reference suddenly dimmed or called into question, individuals find themselves groping for direction, unsure of their bearings and uncertain of their roles.

As has been remarked numerous times, the sense of ecclesial anomie, which has intruded so often into our experience of the past twenty years, contrasts so poignantly with the self-assurance and confident expectation of the years immediately preceding. If I may once more personalize: my first vote in a presidential election was cast for John F. Kennedy in 1960; and my preparation for priesthood took place in Rome during the heady and, in retrospect, halcyon days of Vatican II. The "era of the two Johns" evoked such enthusiasm that the succeeding disenchantment looms all the more striking.

The dispiriting story has been and continues to be

chronicled. Yet most of us require little further commentary upon experiences that are still too vivid, disappointments still too acute, hurts still too raw. What we need, indeed yearn for, is some measure of healing, reconciliation, and redemption: to drink from a Source deeper and purer than the bitter waters which have often been our lot.

In some respects the crisis through which the post-Vatican II Catholic Church is passing through is a crisis of language; and it is strange that its inevitability, whether in a milder or more raging form, had not been foreseen. One does not tamper with a centuries-old language with impunity. And ours was a language culturally forged, liturgically hallowed, educationally reinforced. It articulated a distinctively Catholic identity and allotted individuals specific roles within its monumental enclave. No wonder that tinkering with and then abandoning this language unloosed a flood of neologisms and barbarisms, as well as the occasional poetic utterance.[2]

No group within the Catholic Church was more affected by this linguistic revolution than the priesthood. For the priest was the linguistic practitioner par excellence, the guardian of the sacral language. His expertise was linguistically apparent and his role linguistically founded. It matters not how well or poorly he actually commanded the sacred tongue. To the ears of the profane it could not but seem awesome.

The simple yet complex act of turning this minister of

[2] I have commented upon the post-Vatican II crisis as a "crisis of language" in "Vatican II: Twenty Years Later," *Commonweal*, vol. 109, no. 17 (October 8, 1982). For a "cultural-linguistic" approach to religion and theology, see George Lindbeck, *The Nature of Doctrine* (Philadelphia: Westminster Press, 1984).

the sacred towards the congregation and putting into his mouth words that were no longer archaic and arcane, but ordinary and all too human, effectively shattered a role and called into question an identity. Once the linguistic monopoly was ended, the query was bound to surface: what *does* the priest do that others cannot do? And with much embarrassment many stammered for an answer.

In some ways, our post-Vatican II predicament reminds me of the beginning of Dante's *Divine Comedy*. The poet's authentic awakening was followed by an effort to scale the majestic mountain which he espied, only to learn that this lay beyond his force and required that he first descend into the very depths of the abyss, before he could freely ascend. So the Church, having postponed *aggiornamento* far too long, has come to know, with sorrow and pain, how costly true renewal is and how much stripping bare there must be, before new shoots can sprout from the gnarled yet still vibrant stump. It was and is a wonder-provoking spectacle, especially in a frenetic society grown accustomed to the "quick fix."

Vatican II, however, for all its scarcely-intended shaking of foundations, did mark off parameters for renewal and these remain valid guidelines, tracing the shape of the Church to come.[3] Its liturgical reform brought Word and sacrament, at least potentially, into a new proximity to the whole people and their experience. That people itself was recognized in the more ample ecclesiology of *Lumen Gentium*, the Council's Constitution on the Church, to be

---

[3]Karl Rahner's little book, *The Shape of the Church to Come* (New York: Seabury Press, 1974) remains one of his most accessible and acute writings. Unlike recent American efforts — Eugene Kennedy's *The Now and Future Church* and Mary Durkin and Andrew Greeley's *How to Save the Catholic Church* — it also shows theological depth.

the very substance of Church, whatever further differentiation, within the one people might be required.
Moreover this Church as people of God was set in decisive
dialogue with the world through the Council's pastoral
reflections in *Gaudium et Spes*, its Constitution on the
Church in the Modern World. Such dialogue, the Council
insists, is no luxury, but ingredient to the Church's own
self-understanding.

These undeniable and overdue gains in ecclesiology had
immediate and inevitable implications for ministry. First
and foremost, ministry was rooted firmly within the
matrix of community, not apart from but a part of the
community of God's people which is Church. Second, the
reconstitution of the ordained diaconate as a permanent
ministry within the Church rendered our understanding
of holy orders more supple and demonstrated in practice
that such ministry was perfectly capable of exercise by
married believers. Thirdly, the post-Conciliar institution
of lay ministries by Pope Paul VI in his *motu proprio,
Ministeria Quaedam*, effectively broke the age-old clerical
monopolization of ministry and opened the way for
further important discernment and development.

Many of these practical ministerial advances, exciting
and promising though they be, represent a practice still in
search of a theory. As David Power justly observes: "we
are still in a process of renewal rather than at a point of
arrival."[4] What has become clear to many is that an
adequate theology of ministry depends not merely upon a
renewed ecclesiology (which Vatican II did promote), but
upon a new Christology (for which Vatican II provided
little direction). This emerging conviction found clear

[4]David N. Power, *Gifts That Differ: Lay Ministries Established and Unestablished*
(New York: Pueblo Publishing Co., 1980), p. x.

expression in an address of Archbishop (now Cardinal) Joseph Bernardin on "The Future of Church and Ministry." The Archbishop said: "Christology will be the dominant theological theme in the years immediately ahead. Developments in this field will significantly enrich our understanding of the Church both in terms of how we view its relationship to the Lord and to ourselves, and how we minister in its name."[5] Such Christological reflection proceeds today with great vigor in every quarter of the Catholic world; yet even Schillebeeckx's monumental labors have only resulted in what the author himself labels (with, perhaps, excessive modesty, considering their bulk) a "prolegomenon."[6]

In the meantime, while lay ministries, both formal and informal, develop apace; the ministry of priesthood, already relatively neglected at Vatican II, searches for determinate direction. I certainly do not deny that individual priests have indeed clarified for themselves a meaningful and purposeful role in the religious life of the American Catholic community; but often they do so more by dint of personal strength and creativity than by reflective theological positions. While personal clarification is hard won and commendable, theological articulation is crucial for communal sustenance and testing.

For the crisis of the Catholic priesthood is a corporate phenomenon and it requires a corporate response, both at the level of theory and of practice. Whereas the priest in

[5]Archbishop Joseph L. Bernardin, "The Future of Church and Ministry," *Origins*, vol. 11, no. 47 (May 6, 1982), p. 748.

[6]See his assertion: "Perhaps it will be possible to make a beginning on what is called 'christology' *after* this second volume." Edward Schillebeeckx, *Christ: The Experience of Jesus as Lord* (New York: Seabury Press, 1980), p. 25 (italics in the original).

the pre-Vatican II Church could function and flourish as a single individual, because the Christology which under-girded and the institution which supported his ministry made this stance comprehensible and viable; such is no longer the case. When Christology itself begins to be reconceived in a more corporate and social fashion and when the charismatic factor in the church receives an acknowledged primacy over the institutional factor, then the priesthood itself must be reconceived in corporate and communal terms if it is to be theologically intelligible.[7]

Paradoxically, this growing perception in Christology, ecclesiology, and ministry may coincide with a particularly American sensitivity. Despite America's vaunted and much-maligned "individualism," our nation's religious and political foundation was an act of communal covenanting, classically and magnificently expressed by John Winthrop in his sermon aboard the "Arbella":

> For this end we must be knit together in this work as one man; we must entertain each other in brotherly affection; we must be willing to abridge ourselves of our superfluities for the supply of others' necessities;...we must delight in each other, make others' conditions our own, rejoice together, mourn together, labor and suffer together, always having before our eyes our commission and community in the work, our community as members of the same body, so shall we keep the unity of the Spirit in the bond of peace.
> ("A Modell of Christian Charity")

[7]The modern foundations for such a corporate and charismatic understanding of Christology and ecclesiology were laid, prior to Vatican II, in such works as Emil Mersch's *Theology of the Mystical Body* and Henri de Lubac's *Catholicism: A Study of Dogma in Relation to the Corporate Destiny of Mankind*. A profound contemporary statement is that of Rosemary Haughton, *The Passionate God* (New York: Paulist Press, 1981).

The American experience even to our day seems characterized by the laborious endeavor to make of many one:
e pluribus unum; to realize a community from the many. By
contrast, the European experience, expressed both in
philosophy and in polity, seems much more Platonic in
orientation; *ex uno plures*; the derivation of the many from
the One. Let me attempt to frame this viewpoint in terms
of trinitarian theology. The European angle of vision on
Trinity seems focused upon the "monarchy" of the
Father; the American angle of vision regards with special
concern the communion of the Spirit.[8]

Cognizant, then, of the contemporary context and alert
to possible resources deriving from a peculiarly American
sensitivity, I shall attempt to articulate an approach to
priesthood whose language, while trinitarian (as all com-
prehensive and thus Catholic theology must be), gives
particular emphasis to the Spirit as the "outcome" of
process in God. Communion in the Spirit is the culmina-
tion of God's own inner life and the goal towards which
God's creative, redemptive, and sanctifying action in the
world tends.[9]

[8]The works of John E. Smith offer considerable resources for an American
approach to theological reflection. See, for example, *Themes in American
Philosophy: Purpose, Experience, and Community* (New York: Harper Torch-
books, 1970). One might consult with profit the pioneering essay of Herbert
W. Richardson, *Toward an American Theology* (New York: Harper and Row,
1967).

[9]A first outline of a "pneumatological approach" to theology may be found
in my article, "A New Paradigm for Theology," *The Ecumenist*, vol. 14, no. 6
(September-October, 1976). A pneumatological approach to ordained ministry also characterizes Edward Schillebeeckx, *Ministry: Leadership in the Community of Jesus Christ* (New York: Crossroad, 1981). With regard to
Schillebeeckx one should consult the appreciative, but critical review by
Walter Kasper, "Ministry in the Church: Taking Issue with Edward Schillebeeckx," *Communio*, vol. X, no. 2 (Summer 1983).

II—A Pneumatological Approach to Church and Ministry

Assuming the vantage point of Spirit brings to the fore a number of emphases which, together, can shape the contours of a distinctive approach to Church and ministry. In the first place, the community, endowed with and inspired by the Spirit, becomes the reference point for theological reflection concerning ministry. All ministry, including the ministry of the ordained, finds its proper setting within the community, as further differentiations of the one people of God, richly and diversely gifted with the charisms of the Spirit. Not the least of the merits of the path-breaking "Lima Statement on Ministry," published by the World Council of Churches, is the placement of its reflections upon ministry within "the calling of the whole people of God."[10] In a similar way Vatican II's Constitution on the Church, *Lumen Gentium*, placed its third chapter, "On the Hierarchical Structure of the Church," within the theological context of "The Mystery of the Church" (chapter one) and "The People of God" (chapter two).

Secondly, a Spirit-sensitivity underscores the eschatological nature of Christian faith — the conviction and confession that the last age has dawned in Jesus Christ who is the new, the eschatological Adam (o $\epsilon\sigma\chi\alpha\tau\sigma\sigma$ $A\delta\alpha\mu$ of 1 Cor 15:45) who has become "life-giving Spirit." It has been suggested that the biblical symbol of "Wisdom" refers to the beginning: the Wisdom with which God ordered all things; while the symbol of "Spirit" refers to the consum-

---

[10]See: "Baptism, Eucharist, Ministry," Faith and Order Paper No. 111 (Geneva: World Council of Churches, 1982). The statement was drafted with Roman Catholic participation in the membership of the Commission.

mation: the goal of God's forming and transforming power, now made manifest in Christ and at work in those who believe in Christ's name. Christian faith is caught up in this movement of "the end times": the revelation and realization of God's purpose for the world.

Thus a third element which issues from a Spirit-centered reflection stresses the transformational nature of life in the Spirit. Just as the Spirit conceived the human reality of Jesus, anointed him for his messianic role, and raised his humanity to new and glorious life; so the Spirit, who christens the followers of Christ, transforms their being in the course of their discipleship. In the ancient patristic aphorism, "Christians are made, not born"; and this transformational action is attributed to the personal working of God's Holy Spirit.

The one who is ordained to priesthood within this community of the Spirit is ordered to the building up of *this* community. His leadership, then, is specified by the nature of the community from which he is called and to whose service he is consecrated. Hence it would be ultimately misleading to conceive leadership in the community on either democratic or monarchical models. Rather, the experience of Spirit and its privileged biblical interpretation must guide every effort to understand the nature of ministry and authority within the Church.

In this regard George Tavard makes a persuasive case for locating the focus of such authority in the eucharist. He writes: "ministerial authority is no less and no more than that of the Lord as present in the eucharistic mystery."[11] Though I value Tavard's focus upon the eucharist,

---

[11]George Tavard, *A Theology for Ministry* (Wilmington: Michael Glazier, 1983), p. 132.

I think he risks reducing priestly identity to that of the celebrant of the eucharist, as when he interprets the priestly "character" as "the orientation of the priest toward the eucharist."[12] I myself would prefer to high-light the priest's orientation to the community, which finds fullest expression in the eucharistic celebration. For, though the eucharist celebrates the identity of the community in its most concentrated form, the eucharist itself can only be properly apprehended within the total life of the community, which is a life of ongoing transformation in the Spirit. Perhaps I might hazard this contrast: Tavard's perspective and emphasis appear more Christological, rooted in a theology of the Word; whereas the perspective I am seeking to express is more pneumatological, viewed from the vantage of Spirit.

Nevertheless, though the priest stands solidly within the community, he does so as witness to the transcendent Source and Goal of the community's life. Here Father Tavard offers an illuminating distinction between the ordained minister as "presbyter" and the ordained minister as "priest."[13] It is in the latter capacity that he acts "*in persona Christi*," especially in the celebration of the eucharist. If in the past a wedge had been driven between the ordained acting *in persona Christi* and *in persona ecclesiae*, thereby losing the complex richness of the patristic synthesis, there seems a tendency today to collapse the former into the latter. What is needed is to affirm their inseparability and irreducibility. I think David Power captures the creative tension I am seeking when he writes:

[12]*Ibid.*

[13]*Ibid.*, p. 114.

What the sacrament of order then does is to give the recipient a new role in the life of the church, and, as principal expression of this, a special role in the celebration of the eucharist, where the mystery of the church is celebrated. His position becomes such that in the celebration of the Lord's Supper the relationship to Christ as founder and source of life, as well as the relationship to the community of the apostles and to the communion of all the churches, is expressed and served through his presidency. Because he is empowered to represent the church in this vital action, to represent to it its own very ground of being, we say that he is empowered to represent Christ.[14]

Yet even here the Spirit perspective may provide a unifying focus. For it is Christ, the Giver of the Spirit, who is Lord of the community. To act *in persona Christi*, then, is to act in the name of the Christ who has become life-giving Spirit and who distributes his gifts as he wills, while to act as representative of the Church is to act within that community whose reality is to be a sacrament of the Spirit, being itself transformed and cooperating in the transformation of all created reality.[15]

A final sensitivity which a Spirit-focus will foster and encourage is that of the development of small groups as the unit of ecclesial experience, whether these be called "*comunidades de base*," "grass-roots communities" or "charismatic groups." Without denying different emphases and concerns in the understanding of these groups, I think there is a decisive family resemblance among them. It resides in the experience and conviction that the Spirit

[14]Power, *op. cit.*, p. 127.

[15]The view of Church as "sacrament of Spirit" has been suggested by Walter Kasper (among others). See Kasper's "The Priest's Nature and Ministry: Thoughts on the Future of the Priestly Ministry," in *Faith and the Future* (New York: Crossroad Publishing Co., 1982), p. 78.

acts to bring believers into a face to face encounter wherein their common faith in Christ might be expressed, shared, and strengthened both effectively and affectively, and wherein personal and communal discernment might be supported.

Such gatherings both require and evoke service on the part of the participants. And such service may lead to the discernment of a more formal ministerial call and a commissioning on the part of those who have authority within the community. Among those ministries is that of the ordained priesthood. To clarify the particular character of the ordained priest's service in the Spirit, the third part of this essay is devoted.

III—The Leadership Function of the Ordained Priesthood

Recent studies in ministry have tended to identify the specific charism of the priesthood as that of *leadership*.[16] I have already indicated in a general way my concurrence with this orientation. However, I should like now to spell out more fully my understanding of the peculiar leadership functions incumbent upon the priest. To do so requires insisting upon the peculiar and defining nature of the community from which this ministry comes and to which it is ordered. What is it which identifies the Christian community and differentiates it from other gather-

[16] Besides the works of Power (note 4) and Schillebeeckx (note 9), see also Nathan Mitchell, O.S.B., *Mission and Ministry: History and Theology in the Sacrament of Order* (Wilmington: Michael Glazier, 1982), pp. 301-306; and Thomas Franklin O'Meara, O.P. *Theology of Ministry* (Ramsey, N.J.: Paulist Press, 1983), pp. 201, 202, 209, 210. Tavard, by contrast, acknowledges his own partial dissent from an emerging consensus: *op. cit.*, p. 93 (note).

ings and associations? What are the meanings and values which structure its own self-understanding?

Put most succinctly: the Christian *ekklesia* is the community called into being by God through Christ in the Spirit; a convocation which is, inseparably, a gathering, a building up, and a sending forth. I shall seek to elaborate upon the priest's leadership function, in keeping with this trinitarian pattern of the community's life, by speaking of the priest's mystagogic, Christic, and pneumatic functions. The sense I give to each of these terms will, I hope, emerge in what follows.

1—THE PRIEST'S MYSTAGOGIC FUNCTION

The term "mystagogy" (literally, "leading into the Mystery") was employed in the early Church in relation to the rites of initiation into the Christian community; in particular, the leading of the newly baptized into a deeper knowledge of the mystery of faith which they had experienced in the sacraments of initiation. The bishop himself delivered the mystagogic instruction and served as the preeminent "mystagogue." Perhaps the most celebrated example from the early Church of this episcopal mystagogy are the *Mystagogical Catecheses* attributed to Cyril, Bishop of Jerusalem from 350 A.D.

The term has in our own day been restored to theological usage largely through the labors and sensitivies of Karl Rahner. Rahner rightly saw that encounter with the Mystery who is God lies at the very heart of religious experience and practice. He also perceived that the tendency of technocratic and bureaucratic society to manage or eliminate mystery deprived the Gospel of a vital point of contact in ordinary human experience. Hence

much of Rahner's theological and pastoral effort was
directed both to insisting upon theology's need to respect
the Mystery of God, which can never be comprehended in
our conceptual nets, and to indicating areas of human
experience where we come face to face with mystery.[17]

The term has also been restored to pastoral usage thanks
to its inclusion as one of the stages set forth in the Rite for
the Christian Initiation of Adults. In its epoch-making
restoration of the catechumenate, the document makes
provision for a period of postbaptismal catechesis or
"mystagogia." Once more, as in the early Church, stress is
placed upon the community setting and the experiential
orientation of the process. And once more the bishop is
accorded a decisive role.

Now, in the absence of the bishop, the priest is charged
with particular responsibility for initiating the catechumens; not that the task is uniquely his, but that he bears an
ultimate pastoral responsibility for its order and its outcome.[18] Moreover, this mystagogic function is not limited
to those being initiated for the first time into the Christian
faith; it is exercised vis-à-vis the entire community called
to journey into the inexhaustible Mystery of God.

For the priest to undertake this office with integrity, he
himself must have experienced something of the Mystery
who is the Subject of his preaching, teaching, and witness.
He must have made his own, in whatever contemporary

---

[17]James J. Bacik, *Apologetics and the Eclipse of Mystery: Mystagogy According to
Karl Rahner* (Notre Dame: University of Notre Dame Press, 1980), emphasizes
this important dimension of Rahner's theological investigations.

[18]I stress the close relationship between the episcopal and presbyteral
ministry, to the point of finding Tavard's assertion of their "fundamental
identity" persuasive. See Tavard, *op. cit.*, p. 119; also the more cautious
statement in the Lima document on "Ministry," par. 24.

rhythms and accents, the perennial prayer of the psalmist: "How lovely is your dwelling place, Lord God of hosts" (Ps 84:1); a prayer to which, in Newman's terms, he has given not merely "notional," but "real" assent.

Under this heading of his "mystagogic function," then, the priest is quite simply (though not simplistically) the man *of God*. I believe that this function will once more come to the fore in the ensuing years, in a society increasingly weary of a suffocating one-dimensionality and athirst for the spaciousness of Mystery and worship. By referring to the priest as "man of God," I do not, of course, intend an easy identification, assumed with a clerical collar. This function can only be the fruit of a prolonged wrestling with the Mystery, which, as in the case of Jacob, is bound to leave a mark physical as well as spiritual. Few will attain Augustine's genius of expression. But all should share something of the ongoing quest which finds such splendid utterance in Book Ten of the *Confessions*: "What do I love when I love my God?. . .Late have I loved you, Beauty ever ancient and ever new" (X:6&27).

Further, by his mystagogic sensitivity, the priest will witness to the insufficiency of a reduction of the religious concern, merely to its ethical component. As Kierkegaard insisted, human spiritual development must move beyond the ethical to the religious; it must confront not merely the moral absolute, but the living God. In this regard the priest's function must be that of an advocate of God; and his necessary human advocacy must reach higher and draw deeper than simple humanitarianism. The two great commandments may be inseparable; they are not, however, identical.

An important aspect of the priest's mystagogic function, then, is to be the community's leader of prayer. To be advocate of God is first and foremost to call upon God, to invoke the name of the Holy One, to pronounce blessing and consecration. The leader of prayer must be aware that silence can be as important as words in evoking the awesome Mystery from whom we come and to whom we journey. Moreover, when words are uttered out of this backdrop of reverent silence, they should be words that have a certain "tensive" quality to them, not stereotypical in the manner of the religious cliche.[19] The priest as mystagogue needs be something of a poet, the well-versed practitioner of a language no longer archaic and sacral, but supple and sacramental: revelatory of Hopkins' "dearest freshness deep down things."

When, beginning the community's eucharistic prayer, the priest enjoins: "let us give thanks to the Lord our God," he is both giving expression to a crucial dimension of the eucharist itself and epitomizing the thrust of his own mystagogic function. For, before the Mystery who is God, the only apt human response is one of thanksgiving. Only gratitude answers to grace. The more the priest succeeds in intimating the Mystery, the more will thanksgiving abound.

The priest, as man of prayer, practices the *memoria Dei*, the remembrance of the God who works in nature, in history, and in human lives. The priest, as leader of prayer, invites the community to remember God, to celebrate with thanksgiving what God has done, is doing, and will do. Out of this living memory of priest and people, the Church celebrates its liturgy and remembers in thanksgiv-

[19]John Coulson, *op. cit.*, p. 158f. offers intriguing insights into the nexus between linguistic adequacy and liturgical integrity.

ing the foundational act by which God called and calls it into being: the paschal mystery of Jesus Christ.

2—THE PRIEST'S CHRISTIC FUNCTION

The priest, as man of God, is centered in Jesus Christ, as his remembrance and thanksgiving are specified as the celebration of the eucharistic sacrifice of the Lord. If the priest's mystagogic function is rooted in his experience and appropriation of the beauty of God, his Christic function is founded in his faith-perception of the beauty of God on the face of Jesus Christ.[20] In his own manner and measure, the priest proclaims after Paul: "the light of the knowledge of the glory of God in the face of Christ" (2 Cor 4:6). This is faith matured into knowledge: an affective appreciation of the Mystery made manifest and recapitulated in Christ.

I shall always remember with gratitude a young Mexican seminarian who was studying English at Maryknoll, so that he might then go to Korea and, with his newly acquired English, learn Korean. Astonished by this double dispossession of self, I asked the young man what motivated his commitment. He responded, simply and profoundly: "Soy apasionado de Cristo."

It is such passion for Christ which animates the priest's Christic ministry. To discharge it adequately requires a continuing appropriation of the Christ-mystery. Indispensable here are ongoing scriptural and theological reflection and reading. Such activity certainly includes

[20]The foremost exponent of "a theological aesthetic" is Hans Urs von Balthasar. Consult the helpful collection: *The von Balthasar Reader,* edited by Medard Kehl, S.J. and Werner Loser, S.J. (New York: Crossroad Publishing Co., 1982).

some degree of formal study — whether of scriptural commentaries or theological syntheses. But it also requires a sustained involvement in personal and shared reflection with others engaged in ministry. Ideally, the rectory should provide a context of shared prayer and reflection; and preparation for priesthood should help foster the capacity for such mutual "empowerment" in Christ.[21]

One particularly apt way to foster this growth into the Christ-mystery is through spiritual direction. Spiritual direction concentrates and concretizes the Christic dimension of priestly ministry, both insofar as the priest receives such direction and insofar as he himself serves as spiritual director for others. Such a relationship may, of course, take the classic form of director to directee. But I think it a mistake to neglect the spiritual-direction aspect of so many ministerial encounters: whether preaching, praying, teaching, or counseling.

What I am seeking to underscore in this discussion of the priest's "Christic function" is the radically transformational thrust of Christian faith. The goal of God's redemptive and sanctifying action revealed in Christ is not so much the creation of a new situation, but of a new self. To enter into Christ is to become a "new creation." The Christ-mystery is the establishment of a new humanity, recreated in the image of "the new Adam" who is Jesus Christ.[22]

Two quotes from St. Paul may serve to summarize the

---

[21]Consider the, admittedly, ideal model sketched in the stimulating book of Aaron Milavec, *To Empower as Jesus Did: Acquiring Spiritual Power through Apprenticeship* (New York: The Edward Mellen Press, 1982), pp. 257-262.

[22]Extremely helpful for the structure and dynamics of "transformation" is James E. Loder, *The Transforming Moment* (New York: Harper and Row, 1981).

thrust of this Christic movement. In his *Letter to the Galatians* Paul condenses his personal appropriation of the Gospel in his heart-felt exclamation: "I have been crucified with Christ: it is no longer I who live, but Christ who lives in me" (Gal 2:20). This recentering of the personality in Christ is the vocation to which faith impels us. But what has transpired in the minister is also the credible basis of his ministry. The ministerial concomitant to this personal transformation is expressed by Paul in the same epistle: "I am in travail until Christ be formed in you" (Gal 4:19). The Christic function of the priest's ministry impels the priest, who has come to know the transforming power of Christ, to foster the ongoing transformation of others. Having been empowered by Christ, to empower others in and through Christ.

One might sum up this Christic function of priestly leadership under the rubric of "christening." Just as Christ was anointed, indeed "driven," by the Spirit to undertake his work of reconciliation and at-one-ment, so Christians, baptized into the death of Christ, are sealed with the Spirit of new life and freedom. The priest, who oversees the catechumenate and initiates new members into the community of faith, perceives this ongoing christening process to constitute the heart of his ministry.[23]

Hence priestly ministry is irreducibly sacramental. One can understand the post-Vatican II reaction away from a "merely sacramental" understanding of priestly ministry, in favor of a more "socially involved," less "narrowly ecclesiastical" construal of priesthood. However, the problem with the older model was not its sacramental

---

[23]Confer the Lima statement on "Ministry," par. 30. Many valuable insights may be gleaned from Mark Searle, *Christening: The Making of Christians* (Collegeville: The Liturgical Press, 1980).

insistence, but its deficient sacramentality. Sacraments were divorced from the total life of the community and dissociated from the everyday life of believers. Becoming artificially segregated, they were inevitably privatized.

Sacraments are, instead, highpoints of the christening process, which, of its nature, is ecclesial and hence public. Private masses are profound misnomers; and even private confession is misleading. It is a deeply and defining Catholic sensibility which recognizes that our relation to God is mediated by the community and has repercussions upon the community. Sacraments are key moments in the ongoing process of transformation; moments which promote and empower the christening process that is the heart of discipleship. Sacraments do not canonize the status quo; they call forth the new Christic self, constituted by new relations in the Spirit.[24]

Sacraments, therefore, are, in many respects, countercultural realities. Just as the ancient Christian catechumenate had to combat and counteract many of the values and meanings of the surrounding culture, so the renewal of the catechumenate and the ongoing conversion it initiates must foster the renunciation of many anti-Christian values of the contemporary culture. The sacraments, "rightly administered," cannot fail to denounce a narcissism which denies sin, aging, death, and human need and dependence. They cannot but speak out against cultural "celebrations" and attitudes which are prodigiously wasteful and disdainful of the common good. Sacraments do not pander to private self-fulfillment, but provoke

[24]There are helpful considerations in Regis Duffy, *Real Presence: Worship, Sacraments, and Commitment* (San Francisco: Harper and Row, 1982). See also the concerns expressed by Philip J. Murnion, "A Sacramental Church," *America*, vol. 148, no. 12 (March 26, 1983).

self-transcendence and transformation. Such sacramental consciousness may seem especially counter-cultural in contemporary American society. But, in truth, the sacramental participation in the death of Christ and in the transformed life, which issues only from a faith-filled confrontation with death and the other faces of the Void, must seem scandalous to any society which relies only on its own forces.

The priest as steward of the sacraments is preeminently steward of the eucharist. Here the transformative vision and practice of the Gospel comes to fullest expression. The priest here acts *in persona Christi*, as he presides over the re-presentation of the unique sacrifice of Christ, who offered himself once for all "through the eternal Spirit" (Heb 8:14). In so acting he also stewards the two-fold tradition of this sacrifice: preserving communion with what has been handed down through the ages from the apostles and celebrating communion with all those eucharistic communities throughout the world which constitute the one Church Catholic.

Though the eucharist is a profoundly ecclesial action, it is not for that "unworldly." The eucharist fosters, through the self-offering of the faithful in Christ, the transformation of all created reality. It inspires and effects the vision of a world transformed, a "spiritual body": the fruit of the earth and work of human hands become food and drink in the Spirit. I contend that the authority and responsibility of the bishops of the United States to address questions of social and economic policy (as they have done in their recent pastorals on "Peace" and "the Economy") ultimately rests upon their office as presiders over and stewards of the community's eucharistic celebration. Their concern for the proper setting of the sacramental celebration includes not only the ecclesial but the secular situation. David Power puts it well:

> All has its basis in liturgy, and all has its finality in the transformation of the world. The secular not only need not destroy the eschatological and the mystical: it demands them. The mystical and the eschatological not only do not cause withdrawal from the world: they dictate participation, even while exacting a constant reassessment of such participation.[25]

3—THE PRIEST'S PNEUMATIC FUNCTION

If in the past the ordained effectively monopolized ministry, the pneumatic function of the priest within a community abundantly graced with the gifts of the Spirit will be to discern and coordinate the charisms of the Spirit-endowed people. To preside at the community's eucharist entails also evoking and offering the gifts of the Spirit which are the community's spiritual sacrifice.

The characteristic attitude required for such priestly ministry is that generosity of Spirit manifest in Paul, who exhorts the Corinthians: "I should be pleased for you all to use the tongues of ecstasy, but better pleased for you to prophesy" (1 Cor 14:5); or in Moses who, in the face of Joshua's desire to control the working of the Spirit, exclaimed: "I wish that all the Lord's people were prophets and that the Lord would confer his Spirit on them all" (Num 11:29). The pneumatic function of the ordained greets such outpouring of the Spirit as the enhancement, not the diminution of its own identity. The

[25]Power, *op. cit.*, p. 130.

priesthood of the ordained is fulfilled in evoking the priesthood of the faithful.[26]

The fundamental reason for this is the recognition that Christ-forming is community-forming. The Christ into whom we are christened is the body animated by the Spirit; and its distinctive life is the communion of the Spirit. Such communion is the true gift of the Spirit, the love that seeks and promotes the common good, the end for which God created the universe. It is, therefore, the end to which the mystagogic and the Christic lead: the communion of persons transformed in Christ into a new, liberated creation.

The priest is, radically, the person of communion: the one whose identity is affectively defined by this passion for communion. Though celibacy is not essential to this identity, it can be a powerful sign of it. But it must be a celibacy which is a response to a mystagogic, Christic, and pneumatic vision; not to an institutional requirement alone. I am no prophet (not even of the "minor" stripe), and I cannot predict whether the Church will continue to ask of its candidates for ordination a commitment to a celibate life style. But I think that the community of faith must discern carefully the religious and cultural repercussions of a relaxation of this ancient discipline in a context decidedly unclear about the relation between intimacy and responsibility and dangerously myopic concerning human vocation and destiny.

The pneumatic function of the priest, as the other functions discussed, comes to fullest expression in the eucharistic celebration. The communion which the eucharist effects is the reality toward which the eucharist and

---

[26]See Peter E. Fink, "The Sacrament of Orders: Some Liturgical Reflections," *Worship*, vol. 56, no. 6 (November 1982), pp. 492, 493.

God's whole plan of salvation tends. Union with God through Christ is never absorption or diminution of true personhood. It is communion of persons in the Spirit. The created analogue of the trinitarian Mystery is the whole of redeemed humanity, at-oned in the communion of the Spirit.

The ministerial mode appropriate to such a vision needs to be a communal one. Communion of the Spirit is gift of God; community is the formation which envisions such a transformation. Community cannot guarantee communion; but communion empowers community. Even among presbyters who do not belong to "religious communities," a common prayer seems a necessary condition for the effective exercise of their pneumatic function. Only in such a prayerful environment, for example, will concelebration cease from being a ritual and clerical display and serve its pneumatic function of witness to life in the Spirit.[27]

Finally, pneumatic sensitivity appreciates the reality of ongoing transformation, of recurring tension and struggle as well as present anticipation and enjoyment. In brief, it recognizes and experiences the already/not yet quality of Christian eschatological existence. The whole of *Romans* 8 bears precious testimony to the fact. James Dunn, in summarizing the Pauline understanding, writes:

> For Paul the religious experience of the believer is characterized by paradox and conflict — the paradox of life and

[27]The Lima statement on "Ministry," par. 26 stresses the collegial and communal dimensions of the ordained ministry and its exercise.Noteworthy, in this regard, is the collegial and communal experience enjoyed by the bishops of the United States, meeting for prayer and reflection at St. John's Abbey, Collegeville, from June 12-23, 1982. See the chronicle in *Worship*, vol. 57, no. 1 (January, 1983).

> death, the conflict of Spirit and flesh....It is important to realize that conversion, experience of Spirit, charismatic experience, does not raise the believer above and beyond this conflict — rather the presence and activity of the Spirit sharpens the conflict.[28]

"Spirituality," so popular today and, rightly understood, so integral to the life of Christians, can never be a private preserve, removed from the fray; rather, it inserts individuals and communities into the midst of the fray. . .in the Spirit of Jesus the Christ. Sealed with this Spirit, the ministry and prayer of the priest transpire.

IV—Conclusion

I began this essay with a quotation from Coleridge which extols the benefits of a revolution which issues not in exclusion, but in enlargement. The Catholic people are currently engaged in an ecclesial and ministerial "revolution," which demands our most faith-filled thinking and generous acting. What I have sought to contribute in this essay is not a sociological report, but a personal and theological reflection upon ordained ministry, which seeks to cull experiences and insights of the past twenty years in order to win a perspective and indicate a direction. I hope that the framework offered does not exclude, but enlarges; that it suggests an integration of experience and tradition, of charism and institution, of leadership and office.

[28]James D. G. Dunn, *Jesus and the Spirit* (Philadelphia: Westminster Press, 1975), pp. 338, 339. The theme in the history of spirituality is abundantly illustrated in Aelred Squire, *Asking the Fathers* (London: S.P.C.K., 1973). For a contemporary restatement: Donald Evans, *Struggle and Fulfillment: the Inner Dynamics of Religion and Morality* (Philadelphia: Fortress Press, 1979).

The functions, which I have associated with the ordained priesthood, do not pertain to it in totalitarian fashion. Many aspects are shared, by right and necessity, with other ministries of Word and sacrament: "to equip God's people for work in his service, to the building up of the body of Christ" (Eph 4:12). What I believe to be unique to the ordained is the constellation of functions and their sacramental ordering to leadership service within the community. It is congruent with this that the one so sacramentally ordained preside at the community's sacramental celebration of the eucharist. For both ordination and eucharist attest the objective order of the community whose gathering does not derive from its own initiative and whose continuing nourishment remains sheer grace.[29]

As the community of faith journeys towards the close of the second millennium of Christian history, there are abundant signs of both promise and peril. Certainly, the Lima document on "Ministry," with its rich theology and irenic tone, represents a sign of promise: the possibility of a new unity of mind and heart among all the Christian people. Amongst the perils must be counted that of a totalitarian secularism, restricting religion to an innocuous private preference. Confronted with both promise and peril, the challenge to the churches is to draw more deeply from the wellsprings of their sacramental heritage and consciousness. For sacramentality always bespeaks communal and public action; and whatever enhances authentic sacramentality ultimately subserves the ongo-

[29]For a salutary recovery of the "objectivity of liturgy," see Mark Searle, "Reflections on Liturgical Reform," *Worship*, vol. 56, no. 5 (September 1982), pp. 428, 429. The possibilities of an objectivity founded in tradition, community, and dialogue are explored in Richard Bernstein, *Beyond Objectivism and Relativism: Science, Hermeneutics, and Praxis* (Philadelphia: University of Pennsylvania Press, 1983).

ing transformation of Church and world.

The ordained priesthood in American life today and toward the year 2000 may, with God's grace and mercy, serve the community of faith with renewed vigor as symbol and steward of its own reality as sacrament of the Spirit. In so doing, it may also serve secular society as a sign of its own sacramental possibility. To enact such a compelling vocation, no virtues will be more required than those which Paul, in the context of his "gospel of the Holy Spirit," the eighth chapter of *Romans*, commends to all Christians: hope and patient endurance.

> For we know that the whole of created reality is still groaning in a common travail. And even we ourselves, who have received the Spirit as first fruits of the coming harvest, groan inwardly as we await the full measure of adoption, our whole body's liberation. For, though we have been saved, it is in hope. Now hope does not exist if its object is in view. Why hope for what one sees? But if, indeed, we hope for what we do not yet see, then we await it with patient endurance.   (Rom 8:22-25)

American Sisters Now

Marie Augusta Neal, S.N.D. de Namur

Is she a nun?

I do not know. How can you tell anymore?

How could you tell before?

It was easy. She wore the habit, lived in a convent, observed the cloister. When you met her on the street, there were always two. They were quiet, spent most of their time in chapel, attended liturgy daily and lived what was called the regular life. They did not eat in public nor attend the theatre except with their students; taught girls more than boys; staffed hospitals, schools, orphanages, homes for the elderly, and academies for girls where the latter became young ladies. They were known to be very obedient to their superiors whom they often called "Mother," and, when you talked to them, they did not seem to be aware of what was really happening politically, nor even to care. They did not read newspapers or watch television or get involved in the resolution of social problems. They were quite naive about shopping and handling money. Often they were really good at what they did, but the concerns of the day were not their concerns. In sum, they were other-worldly. They seemed to be closer to God than to other people and their God seemed quite far away. Heaven was more important to them than earth. Or so it seemed.

I think you are confusing nuns and sisters.

Is there a difference? I am only saying what I have observed. I think the names are used interchangeably.

They are, but in fact they refer to two different vocations in the Church. Nuns live a cloistered life in monasteries or convents. They recite the daily hours of the liturgy, spend many hours in meditation, spiritual reading, and do only work necessary to support themselves, work that does not distract them from this life of prayer in union with God (*Sponsa Christi*, 1950). Sisters, on the contrary, choose a life of service to neighbors with needs, needs ranging over the fields of education, health, and other human services, as well as religious education and missionary work. They have an apostolic spirituality adjusted to the effective carrying out of these various services. They take simple rather than solemn vows and they are expected to adapt their life of prayer to the requirements of their ministries to people rather than to the restrictions of the cloister. The reason you get them confused with nuns is that the church did also, prior to the renewal of the Second Vatican Council and, in some respects, still does.

Because of reasons too complex to recount here (Neal, Orbis, 1985), clear differentiation of sisters from nuns has occurred in the two decades since the Second Vatican Council. The life of the cloistered nun still continues with its centuries-long emphasis on the singing of the liturgy of the hours and the long periods of reflective meditation and spiritual reading in the monastery, separated from the outside world by wall and cloister. That age-old calling for monks and nuns to go apart is still in place. What has changed is the assigning of the same life style to sisters collaborating with other concerned people in the work of addressing human problems of ignorance, illness, and evil.

Women in the Church, from the very early Christian times, have had to address challenges to their felt calls to do God's will in a gospel context in the world. The regulation of the vocations of widows, virgins, deaconesses, hermits, nuns and sisters is part of the long history of women in church-related roles (McNamara, Fiorenza 1983). However, it is sisters particularly who today receive public attention and of whom an account is requested because of the striking changes observable since Vatican II in their life styles and mission commitment. For the most part, for them, the cloister, the convent, the religious habit, the silence, and the regular life are gone, or at least are so modified that they are no longer visible as criteria for identification. In their place has come public witness to unjust conditions of society, even to the point of risk of life. Today Maura Clark, Ita Ford, Dorothy Kazel and Jeanne Donovan, two Maryknoll sisters, an Ursuline sister and a lay woman volunteer, all of whom risked and lost their lives in providing human services to the poor in a revolutionary setting, model for us typical sister behavior but raise the question of what has caused the change.

Factors Leading Up to the Changes

As early as 1929, Pope Pius XI raised the justice question of the adequacy of sisters' professional preparation for the teaching they were doing. He recommended training to competency (Pius XI). In 1950, there was great activity among religious congregations of women as heads of these groups were called to Rome for a series of international meetings which resulted in the founding of regional councils of "Mother Generals", formation personnel and educators toward the professional updating of the training of sisters for their ministries among the people (Myers, Kolmer). The founding of the Conference of Major Superiors of Religious Women (CMSW) and of the Sister Formation Conference is the form this early renewal took in the United States (Kolmer). As a result of these actions, heads of congregations began comparing notes and examining their procedures, and younger members of most religious congregations of sisters began studying modern theologies and getting academic credentials at Catholic universities while living in houses of study on university campuses. All this was happening during the civil rights activity of the fifties and the third world movements and anti-war movement of the sixties (Muckenhirn, Myers).

During the same period, the Vatican urged religious congregations of women to allocate 10% of their growing membership to missionary activity in foreign third world countries; and in Latin America, as well as in Africa, local movements against oppressive colonial structures were not only in progress but were receiving some considerable Church support in their incipient stages. This support was dividing the local churches and bringing the sisters in contact with lay activists for human liberation, but it was alive with gospel content.[1] Preparation for the Second

[1]Besides Paulo Freire's, *Pedagogy of the Oppressed*, the main sources for this information are the several publications of Maryknoll's Orbis Books. See

Vatican Council, called by Pope John XXIII just after he completed *Pacem In Terris*, in which he announced that peace, poverty, and human rights are the central concerns of the committed Catholic, found the sisters ready to respond even to the somewhat patronizing invitation of Cardinal Suenens' *Nun in the World* (1963) to update their congregational structures in preparation for this promising new mission of the Church (Muckenhirn, Myers, Grollmes). This mission, formalized at Vatican II, preceded that Council in social action and theological reflection. It was and still is an invitation to powerless peoples to share access to the growing material goods that provide life and to all peoples to oppose the production of material goods that bring death — weapons, nuclear waste, and other environmental hazards. It is yielding fruit in the mid-eighties in the corporate preparation and teaching of the bishops' pastorals on war and peace, and on the economy (see *Origins*, Oct. 28, 1982; Nov. 15, 1984. See also: Hertzog, Richard, Santa Ana, Neal, Baum, Cabestrero 1977.)

The Decree on Renewal of Religious Life, a document of the Second Vatican Council, mandating a review and revision of all aspects of life in vows in the Church, did not take most religious orders of women by surprise, though it is true that some did not even know it was promulgated for them, so other-worldly was their focus.[2] The decree

especially Berryman, Cussianovich, Dorr, Eagleson, Gutierrez, Hanks. Berryman is the best source for describing how basic Christian communities function.

[2]All the opinions attributed to sisters in this essay are derived from the Sisters' Survey of 1967 and its retest in 1980. The data concerning structures and changes in structures are taken from the congregational survey of 1966 and its retest in 1982. The latter study is published in Neal's *Catholic Sisters in Transition from the 1960s to the 1980s*, Michael Glazier Inc., 1984. Segments of

mandated the calling of special general chapters for the updating of constitutions to make them effective instruments for the implementation of the new directions embodied in the Council documents (Flannery).

From 1966 onward through 1984, sisters' congregations engaged all their members, as mandated by the Decree on Renewal of Religious Life, in the active review and revision of their end and spirit, formation programs, government structures, life styles and practice of the vows (see Flannery, p. 612-613). The revisions were formalized in new constitutions, after they were planned, deliberated and accepted in General Chapters to which elected delegates from the membership were sent for this very purpose. Twenty years of experimentation and evaluation were devoted to the preparation of these documents (Neal, 1984).

Because of their increased knowledge of modern theology, their developed educational programs for ministry preparation, their reading and reflecting on the conditions

the 1967 survey are presented in *The Proceedings of the Conference of Major Superiors of Women Religious* for 1966, 1967, and 1968 and in several journal articles listed in the references: Neal, 1970, 1971a and 1971b, 1975. One summary of the 1980 survey is reported in *Probe*, May-June, 1981. A book and a monograph are currently in preparation reporting on these data in a more complete form. The Sisters' Survey of 1967 was a population study of sisters in the United States, studying their readiness for the implementation of the decrees of Vatican II. It included 139,000 sisters, each responding to 649 questions. Eighty-eight percent of all those contacted responded. The retest in 1980 was a random sample of 3740 sisters. A total of 65% of all those contacted answered 428 questions, 175 of which were retests of the 1967 items. All four studies were sponsored by the Leadership Conference of Women Religious and all participating groups. This was later made available to everyone. It is the Glazier publication mentioned above. One other piece of research in this series is a content analysis of the chapter decrees of 280 of these congregations completed in 1974. In that study each congregation received a comparative analysis of its findings with a national profile.

of the times, as recommended by the renewal documents, and the application of these new understandings to their on-going ministries, sisters incorporated, to a remarkable degree, the new social agenda of the Church into their formal statements of mission and into their work. The combined activity of revising constitutions and experimenting with the new direction of mission opened their consciousness to the realities of the sufferings and burdens of the struggling poor, locally and globally, in ways that cannot now be erased (Cussianovich). This social agenda itself was growing out of the mandates of Vatican II's Pastoral Constitution of the Church in the Modern World and subsequent Church documents, particularly *The Development of Peoples*, 1967; *The Call to Action*, 1971; and the Synod document: *Justice in the World*, 1971. (See O'Brien for a collection of these documents). In 1972, in *Evangelica Testificatio*, Pope Paul VI directed religious to implement *The Call to Action* letter of 1971. It gave a direct mandate to religious to be in the forefront of this action for justice and peace. The challenge given at that time received direct and serious response from sisters (cf. LCWR, 1974).

What was unique about what the sisters accomplished in the renewal years was the application of what they learned from listening to each other recount the struggles of the people among whom they lived and worked, especially what they learned from sisters in missionary countries and in poverty areas of the United States. Sister delegates   chapters from Brazil, Peru, Central America, Zaire, Sou. 1 Africa, Chile, Nigeria, Kenya and Southeast Asia, as well as from the inner cities of the United States, Appalachia and other poor rural areas of the South, and especially after the publication of the bishops' pastoral, *This Land is Home to Me*, were heard, in many cases for the first time, in the context of planning more effective ways of doing the mission and structuring their communal life to do it more humanely and effectively.

The ecumenical movement had its deep influence also. Prior to Vatican II, most sisters did their ministry in isolation even from other Church workers doing the same service to the poor in the same area of the city, so strictly was cloister observed. Invited to work together during the civil rights movement, they experienced a community of faith that transformed their ministries. These experiences were shared in chapter and became a significant part of programs for review of the effectiveness of ministry. Reviewing yearly and experimenting with what they had deliberated through several sessions of special general chapters devoted to the agenda of renewal, the sisters' new understanding of human needs, examined in the light of the gospel, came to inform their choices of congregational structures.

The conscientization methods, learned in basic Christian communities especially in Brazil, of acting and reflecting on the consequence of programs to eliminate a perceived oppression, were discussed at chapters and incorporated into procedures for learning and planning (Freire, Berryman).

The new choice was expressed in these words: a special option for the poor (Dorr). Granted that many religious congregations were explicitly founded to help the poor either through a ministry of educating poor children, opening foundling homes, or beginning nursing services, the fact is that in 1967 when asked: have you ever worked with the materially poor? 83% of the 139,000 sisters who responded to the Sisters' Survey, that is 88% of all sisters contacted at that time, had to say they did not work with the poor, and 57% said in fact they never had done so. In the old traditions built up before the Council, that was not seen as a deflection from the original mission because lack of knowledge of the faith was defined as spiritual poverty and hence working for those who experienced it, a worthy ministry. There was relatively little shared understanding at that time about how social structures, even those within churches, co-opt the energies and dedication of religiously committed groups to works that had lost their apostolic charism and in some cases never even had such a quality to begin with. The renewal brought more shared understanding of this social phenomenon and more carefully constructed guidelines for choice and action to protect against its recurrence (Holland and Henriot, Eagleson and Scharper, Neal, 1977).

As sisters asked themselves what effect their ministry in education, health services and other works had on the quality of life in their society, prompted by the social justice themes in the renewed church, they assessed the effects of their ministry on the life chances of the poor. They concluded that the doing of good works needed to be informed with a transforming mission. This meant that education, health work and other services required a critical perspective that comes from an experience of sharing in the making of informed decisions, sharing in carrying them out, and sharing responsibility for the consequences. This discovery led sisters to revise their methods of government from forms that fostered dependency and childlikeness to forms that fostered responsible accountability for corporate as well as individual decisions. This area of government for mission is the most radical change in the structures of religious congregations of Catholic women and involves some 90% of all sisters in the United States.[3]

[3]This is derived from item 418 of the 1980 survey. A copy of this instrument can be procured from the author.

Reflection on the mission in the light of the new social justice agenda of the church then led to some of the major revisions sisters opted for in their new constitutions: (1) the elimination of cloister and the welcoming of local community people to share meals, prayer and discussion, while at the same time preserving that privacy needed to continue a life of contemplative apostolic spirituality; (2) the simplification of the schedule for prayer and meditation, not decreasing it but making it more flexible regarding time and more open to participation with colleagues, while preserving periods set aside for retreat and private prayer, even more needed now in this more public life; (3) the reduction of the religious habit to simple ordinary clothing and the wearing of a cross or other symbol characteristic of the tradition of the specific congregation, to enable a more participative relationship with others working toward common goals; (4) a widening of choice of ministry for individual sisters from assignment to jobs within existing educational, health, and other institutions serving the Catholic community to a process of discernment around the mission of the congregation as expressed in its documents and the specific abilities and religious aspirations of individual members; and (5) the choice of government forms that allowed full participation of all members in the decisions the community makes about mission, life style, life of prayer and purpose, befitting a community of women bonded together to be of service following a biblical perspective.

It would be ignorance of the history of religious life in the Church to think that all these changes were merely a modern initiative. On the contrary, they are for the most part, the realization of an initiative verbalized by St. Vincent de Paul, when in 1634 he and Louise de Marillac were envisioning the life style of the Sisters of Charity for the effective doing of their mission to alleviate the results of poverty. In summarizing what the life should be like in comparison with the style of the previous three hundred years of cloister, he said:

> The sisters should have no convent but a hospital, houses of the sick, or an asylum; no cell but a hired room, no chapel but the parish church, no cloister but the streets of the town; for enclosure they have only obedience, for a grille, the fear of God, for a veil, holy modesty.[4]

Today the mission itself is taking another transition that has called sisters to new ingenuity for its realization. The justice and peace agenda include the alleviation of the results of poverty but it does not end there. Given the reality of modern technology for producing food and means of durable shelter, we can now think in terms of providing food, clothing and shelter for the whole human race. The problem is now no longer the inevitability of malnutrition, epidemics, and exposure to the destructive forces of nature; rather it is the social problem that these destructions of human life still continue when we have the resources to eliminate the causes of poverty (Lappe and Collins, Avila, Murphy, 1983, 1984, Bouvier). The Church calls us to solidarity with the poor because together we can provide for human need. As Church, we begin to sense the newness of this agenda. In the words of Pope Paul VI:

> You hear rising up, more pressing than ever, from their personal distress and collective misery, "the cry of the poor." Was it not in order to respond to their appeal as God's

[4]This is recorded in St. Vincent's letters to the Daughters of Charity.

privileged ones that Christ came? In a world experiencing the full flood of development this persistence of poverty-stricken masses and individuals constitutes a pressing call for "conversion of minds and attitudes," especially for you who follow Christ more closely in this earthly condition of self-emptying. (Paul VI, *Evangelica Testificatio* #17)

Vows

Sisters all over the world are trying to answer this call to love and to do it through the radical living of the vows of poverty, chastity and obedience. The vow of poverty, the first in focus to realize this mission of changed structures, challenges them to simplicity of life style and a full sharing of their trained talents to service human needs; their vow of chastity, to be celibate for the sake of the kingdom; and obedience, to do the will of God as did Jesus and in the light of the signs of the times. The new emphasis of the vows is clear in new Constitutions and in newly expressed vow formulas. The commitment to the vowed life is one of the strongest held convictions of sisters in the 1980s.[5]

Problems

Each new era in the development of religious life has had its own tensions and problems. This one is no exception. The problem of gravest concern is that of numbers.

[5]Eighty-six percent of the responders felt that they personally experienced a quality of commitment that distinguishes the religious vocation from other callings, and 60% had no doubts about this commitment at all (Item 424, 1980).

The number of sisters entering religious life today is only 15% of what is was in 1966. That does not mean there will be no one left to do the work. Since Vatican II, the laity have been more responsive to the invitation of Jesus to respond to the corporate mission of the Church because, for the first time, they are recognized as peers in the doing of the mission and they are responding as peers. They are less docile, more creative, more committed and more enthusiastic (Vaillancourt). In fact, it is, in all likelihood the maturing of the role of the laity in the Church that has emphasized the true functions of vowed women and men in the Church, as they yield their monopolies on certain administrative and service functions to their lay colleagues. The struggle over division of labor holds up choice to join religious communities (Fiorenza 1981).

In another direction, it is probably the fact that the religious of the future will be drawn more numerously from the Catholics of the future, namely Latin Americans, Africans and Asians, the growing Catholic peoples of the world. This fact makes the review of structures essential at this time. Customs deeply rooted in a European medieval life style are quite meaningless to young people from these backgrounds and who are bent on following Jesus in his mission to the poor. Just as the dress of the old religious congregations was originally the contemporary dress of ladies or peasants, depending on which level of society the founders came from, so today, the dress will be once again the dress of the people hearing God's call and deciding to make a generous response. Dress, however, for religious in the United States at the present time, is not an important issue any more. It was in 1967 because it was symbolic of the security of the whole institution of religious life.

Today, religious life for women is focused more on the realization of the mission.[6]

Government continues to be a problem for several reasons: (1) full participation in decision-making takes more time than many women want to expend on planning; (2) it is not easy to have to take seriously every expressed point of view; (3) the world one comes to know through participation is often more complex than one's conservative tendencies would like to think it is; (4) when one does not know what is going on, one can think God intervenes more directly than social analysis demonstrates to be so; (5) the search for God's will involves more secular knowledge than many choose to have; (6) outdated theologies are demonstrably so when knowledge of the life chances of the poor are known; (7) the established Church does not yet fully appreciate this focus of government.[7]

There is a strong affirmation among congregations of sisters today for the new emphasis in the Church on a biblical spirituality. Reflection on biblical materials is much higher now than it was in 1967, while the emphasis on prayer and meditation has remained high. The focus on mission seems to have enhanced a contemplative spirituality while adding an apostolic dimension to it.

[6]In 1980, 90% of the sisters surveyed acknowledged that addressing the causes of the poverty of the poor, as well as serving their needs was part of their ministry and/or incorporated into their constitutions as part of their mission (Item 403, 1980). In contrast, only 1% of the sisters surveyed in 1980 felt that all sisters should wear a religious habit; and only 7% that they should return to it now (Item 419, 1980).

[7]There is no structural reason why the govenments of religious congregations of women need be modeled on hierarchy. Vowed women do not belong to the clerical orders. Most religious women understand this distinction today.

Being a sister today in the Church is a challenging and sobering experience. Like other adults who have tried living in communes and taking each other seriously as peers, sisters are discovering how much control, humor, and loving concern are needed to enable them to live as peers and not in roles of mothers and daughters, artificially contrived to retain the discipline of regular life (Kanter). Sisters are also finding that the experience of small-group living is worth the effort, especially when one tries to counsel others toward conflict resolution when the problematic conflict is centered within small groups. One's own experience then is a living witness to trying to live as Jesus did, in a witness of gentleness and compassion, with fuller social awareness of the potential of holy things being co-opted for pragmatic ends, and a deep commitment to altruism as a gospel mandate.

Is she a sister?

Yes, I think she is.

How do you know?

She really believes God dwells with the poor. She is committed to bringing about the reign of God which she believes is reflected in human behavior. Even though she knows it is a future reality, she believes she has a role in bringing it about.

But that is the work that Jesus did. I know and so does she (Sloyan, 1984).

So why the vows?

It is a risk of life and the vows are her support. The sister does what she can. Her soul is at peace; her heart is light. She is a professional, committed to the transformation of the world, living in solidarity with the poor, in a community with a simple life style. When others move on, she can stay. When it is time to go, she can leave.

There is always another community to join, more work to be done, and sisters to support her in her commitment to the poor. It is not a glamorous calling but it is a way to do God's will in a congregation with a mission, in a Church that is biblically based.

Bibliography

Avila, Charles. *Ownership*. Maryknoll, New York: , Orbis Books, 1983; London: Sheed and Ward.

Baum, Gregory. *The Priority of Labor*. New York: Paulist Press, 1982.

Berryman, Phillip. *Religious Roots of Rebellion*.Maryknoll, New York:, 1984.

Bouvier, Leon F. *Planet Earth 1984-2034: A Demographic Vision*. Population Bulletin. Vol. 39. No. 1. Population Reference Bureau, Washington D.C., 1984.

Cabestrero, Teofilo. *Ministers of God, Ministers of the People*. Maryknoll, New York: Orbis Books, 1983.

Cardenal, Ernesto. *The Gospel of Solentiname*. Maryknoll, York: Orbis Books, 1976.

Cussianovich, Alejandro. *Religious Life and the Poor: Liberation Theology Perspectives*. Maryknoll, New York: Orbis Books, 1979.

Dorr, Donal. *Option for the Poor: A Hundred Years of Vatican Social Teaching*. Maryknoll, New York: Orbis Books, 1983.

Eagleson, John and Philip Scharper. ed. *Puebla and Beyond: Documents and Commentary on Meetings of the the National Conference of Latin American Bishops, 1977*. Maryknoll, New York: Orbis Books, 1979.

Fiorenza, Elizabeth Schüssler, *In Memory of Her: a Feminist Theological Reconstruction of Christian Origins*. New York: Crossroads, 1983.

Fiorenza, Elizabeth Schussler, "Lay Women and Nun Women," *Probe*, 1981.

Flannery, Austin, *Vatican Council II: The Conciliar and Post Conciliar Documents*. Newport, New York: Costello Pub. Co. 1975.

Freire, Paulo. *Pedagogy of the Oppressed.* New York: Seabury Press, 1970.

Grollmes, Eugene, M. *Vows But No Walls: An Analysis of Religious Life*. St. Louis: B. Herder Book Co., 1967.

Gutierrez, Gustavo. *The Power of the Poor in History*. Maryknoll, New York: Orbis Books, 1983.

Hanks, Thomas D. *God So Loved the Third World: The Bible, Reformation, and Liberation Theology*. Maryknoll, New York: Orbis Books, 1983.

Holland, Joe and Peter Henriot. *Social Analysis: Linking Faith and Justice*. rev.ed. Maryknoll, New York: Orbis Books, 1983.

Herzog, Frederick. *Justice Church: New Function of the Church in North American Christianity*. Maryknoll, New York: Orbis Books, 1980.

Kanter, Rosabeth. *Commitment and Community*. Cambridge: Harvard University Press, 1972.

Kolmer, Elizabeth. *Religious Women in the United States: A Survey of Influential Literature from 1950-1983*. Wilmington, Delaware: Michael Glazier Inc., 1984.

Lappe, Frances Moore, Joseph Collins. *Food First, Beyond the Myth of Scarcity*. Boston: Houghton Mifflin, 1977.

LCWR, *Widening the Dialogue: Reflections on "Evangel-*

ica Testificatio." Washington, D.C.: Leadership Conference of Women Religious, 1974.

McNamara, Jo Ann. *A New Song. The Origins of the Community of Virgins in the First Three Centuries.* New York: Haworth Press, 1983.

Murphy, Elaine M. "The Environment to Come: A Global Summary." Population Reference Bureau, Washington, D.C., 1983.

Murphy, Elaine M. "Food and Population: A Global Concern." Population Bureau, Washington, D.C. 1984.

Muckenhirn, Sister M. C.B. ed. *The Changing Sister.* Notre Dame, Indiana: Fides Publishing Co., 1965.

Muckenhirn, Sister M.C.B. *The New Nuns.* New York: The New American Library, 1967.

Myers, Sister Bertrand. *Sisters for the Twenty-First Century.* New York: Sheed and Ward. 1965.

Neal, Marie Augusta. *Catholic Sisters in Transition from the 1960s to the 1980s.* Wilmington, Delaware: Michael Glazier, Inc., 1984.

Neal, Marie Augusta. *A Sociotheology of Letting Go: A First World Church Facing Third World People.* New York: Paulist Press, 1977.

Neal, Marie Augusta. "A Theoretical Analysis of Renewal in Religious Orders in the U.S.A.," *Social Compass.* Vol.xviii, 1971, 7-27.

Neal, Marie Augusta, "The Relation between Religious Belief and Structural Change in Religious Orders," *Review of Religious Research.* Part I, Vol XII, No. I Fall, 1970, 2-16; Part II, No. 3, Spring, 1971, 154-164.

Neal, Marie Augusta, "Cultural patterns and Behavioral Outcomes in Religious Systems: a study of religious orders of women in the United States," Lille, France: International Conference of Sociology of Religion 1975, 59-77.

O'Brien, David and Thomas A. Shannon. *Renewing the Earth: Catholic Documents on Peace, Justice and Liberation*. Garden City, New York: Doubleday Image Book, 1977.

Richard et al. *Idols of Death and the God of Life: A Theology*. Maryknoll, New York: Orbis Books, 1983.

Santa Ana de, Julio. *Towards a Church of the Poor*. Maryknoll, New York: Orbis Books, 1979.

Sloyan, Gerard S. *Jesus in Focus: A Life in Its Setting*. Mystic, Connecticut. Twenty Third Publication, 1983.

Suenens, Leon Joseph Cardinal. *The Nun in the World: Religious and the Apostolate*. Westminster, Maryland: Newman Press. 1963.

Vaillancourt, Jean-Guy. *Papal Power: A Study of Vatican Council over Lay Catholic Elites*. Berkeley, California: University of California Press. 1980.

Church Documents

National Council of Catholic Bishops. "The Challenge of Peace; God's Promise and Our Response," *Origins*. October 28, 1982, Vol. 12: No 20.

National Council of Catholic Bishops. "Catholic Social Teaching and the U.S. Economy," draft 1. *Origins*. November 15, 1984. Vol. 14: No. 22/23.

Pope Leo XIII, *Rerum Novarum*, 1981, Washington D.C.; National Catholic Welfare Conference, 1942.

Pope Pius XI, *Christian Education of Youth*. 1929, Boston: St. Paul Editions.

Pope Pius XI, *Quadragesimo Anno*, 1931, Washington, D.C.: National Catholic Welfare Conference, 1942.

Pope Pius XII. *Sponsa Christi*, 1950. Boston: St. Paul Editions.

Pope John XXIII, *Mater et Magistra*, 1961, New York: The America Press.

Pope John XXIII, *Pacem in Terris*, 1963, Boston: St. Paul Editions.

Pope Paul VI, *Pastoral Constitution on the Church in the Modern World*, 1965, Boston: St. Paul Editions.

Pope Paul VI, *Populorum Progressio*, 1967, Boston: St. Paul Editions.

Pope Paul VI, *A Call to Action*, 1971, Washington, D.C.: United States Catholic Conference.

Pope Paul VI, *Evangelica Testificatio*, 1971. Boston: St. Paul Editions.

Pope John Paul II, *Laborem Exercens*, 1981, Boston: St. Paul Editions.

Synod of Bishops, *Justice in the World*, 1971, Boston: St. Paul Editions.

Bishops of Appalachia, *This Land Is Home to Me*, 1975, Prestonsburg, Kentucky: Catholic Committee of Appalachia.

Vatican Council II, *Decree on Renewal of Religious Life*. Glen Rock, New Jersey: Paulist Press, 1966.

Giving Praise and Thanks

⮜ ✳ ⮞

Kathleen Hughes, R.S.C.J.

"We thank you for counting us worthy to stand in your presence and serve you." from *Eucharistic Prayer II*

Introduction

What a delight to receive an invitation "to write happily about matters liturgical." What a lovely idea to gain perspective on these last twenty years of liturgical renewal by stepping back and recognizing the extraordinary progress which has been made. What a joy to abandon, albeit briefly, a more fashionable, critical stance vis à vis the liturgy and to glory in its many successes and even more numerous signs of hope.

It is so easy to fire salvos at the liturgy. Most of us, amateur and professional liturgists alike, are highly critical of the liturgical life of the Church. It is an event about which we positively surprise ourselves when we feel so strongly, when normally mild-mannered individuals lose all control in a discussion. Yet, the very heat generated in liturgical discussions is in itself a splendid sign of the love with which the liturgy is held; it attests to the awareness, rooted deeply in our hearts, that since we have been counted worthy to stand in God's presence and serve, we ought to do it well.

It will be my thesis in the balance of this essay that the liturgical renewal mandated by Vatican Council II has been happily launched in the American Church, I suspect even beyond the optimistic expectations of the Council Fathers. Perhaps never before in the history of the Church has so much been accomplished in so short a time as has the radical transformation of our way of worship. In the American Church, if not in the Church universal, these changes have been greeted with acceptance by nearly all and with enthusiasm on the part of many. We have much for which to be thankful. And because thanksgiving seems to me an appropriate response, I would like to structure my reflections according to the several parts of our great prayer of praise and thanksgiving, the Eucharistic Prayer. The chief elements of that prayer, thanksgiving, acclamation, epiclesis, narrative of institution and consecration, anamnesis, offering, intercessions and a final doxology, will provide the pattern for this essay. I trust that the meaning of these elements of prayer will become clear as we proceed.

Thanksgiving

The Eucharistic Prayer begins appropriately by focusing the attention of the community on the goodness and faithfulness of God. In the name of the whole community, the presider gives thanks for the mighty acts of God and particularly for some special aspect of the work of salvation as appropriate to the day, the feast or the liturgical season.

As we examine the state of liturgical renewal there are, indeed, many concrete reasons to give thanks, many quite remarkable strides which we have taken to worship more nearly "in spirit and in truth."

"Participation" is a word which gathers up a number of radical changes in the way in which we understand our role in liturgy. Participation was signalled as the celebrant moved to the far side of the altar, facing the congregation and symbolically suggesting the community's role as co-celebrants at the altar. In taking those few short steps around to the far side of the altar, the priest has moved from the position of mediation to that of invitation, if you will, drawing out the community's response through admonitions, dialogues, gestures and prayers on its behalf. No longer was the community to be spectator at a sacred drama taking place at some distance. The re-orientation of the altar and the celebrant in relationship to the community made clear how important it is that each one participate in the liturgy according to his or her role in the assembly.

The participation of members of the assembly has taken many forms. Certainly there is a profound sense, expressed in the Constitution on the Sacred Liturgy and encouraged in the renewed rites, that each Christian as member of the "royal priesthood" of Christ is called to full, conscious and active participation in the celebration. Such participation is demanded by the nature of liturgy and is both the right and the obligation of one so called to share in the priesthood of Christ. Such active participation might appropriately be designated as one of many ministries within the assembly.

Beyond the "ministry of participation" to which we have been called by virtue of our baptism, more and more men and women have placed themselves at the service of the liturgical life of the community in other forms of service. Ministries of word, music, hospitality, altar and communion assistance are attracting many members of local parishes. As a community we have come to recognize that ministry is a function of need and that the community has need of well-prepared readings, carefully chosen music, a gracious welcome, and so on. Furthermore, it has become increasingly apparent that planning has emerged as yet another liturgical ministry, meeting the deep-seated need in each community for services of prayer which touch the real life experience of those who assemble for prayer.

Careful planning, born in prayer and nourished by a deep knowledge of the community and a love of the community's tradition (both the history and the theology of the way we have prayed over the centuries), offers us another reason to give praise and thanks, because by and large the days of "tinkering" are over. Rare now are those eager experiments hot off the Xerox machine. The dust has settled on novelty, and novelty has yielded to a profound respect and love for the tradition and a peace-filled effort first to master what is already in the books before making up liturgies ex nihilo.

The era of the amateur is departing along with "tinkering." There were moments in our recent past when the amateur was crowned, perhaps in some measure because we misunderstood that ministry was *not* a question of democracy but rather included an obligation to discern gifts among ourselves and affirm and train gifted persons to the service of the community. In our haste to get on with the renewal we spent neither the time to train ministers nor the money to hire professionals, a situation which continues to exist in some dioceses, but fewer than even ten years ago. Training programs, workshops, and seminars abound. Communities across the country have recognized the speed with which the whole renewal was introduced and have called a healthy halt to a "type A personality" approach in favor of a more measured procedure. Because of the outstanding work of certain liturgical centers such as Notre Dame, Catholic University, and St. John's in Collegeville, the country has a pool of professionals working now at the diocesan and local levels to assist the further implementation of the reform.

Yet another reason to give thanks is the community's rediscovery of its need for a variety of celebrations to nourish its life of faith. In the immediate post-Vatican II era all devotions disappeared, because they were somehow understood to be out of place or at least slightly embarrassing. Novenas, missions, rosaries, forty hours, benediction, May crownings...we could go on and on. Almost overnight devotions went the way of the Edsel, too outmoded to be driven around town, but "polished secretly in one's garage" by those who loved them! For a few years after the Council Catholic piety was nourished almost exclusively by the eucharistic celebration, a situation impossible to sustain for long, as the history of Christian spirituality could quickly demonstrate. Happily, parishes are once again willing to supplement the eucharistic life of the community, but now with "devotions" geared to the chief seasons of the church year and shaped by sound liturgical principles. Lent is increasingly celebrated, as the community's long retreat. In accord with ancient history Lent is the season which helps us to recognize that we belong to an "order of penitents," in need of conversion and new life. Communities with catechumens in their midst are particularly enriched throughout the Lenten and Easter season by gatherings for reflection and prayer which focus on the journey of conversion all of us have embarked upon together. The Advent and Christmas season has also been recovered as a time of rich meaning, a time when past, present and future merge in the community's longing for the presence of God-with-us.

Other sacramental and liturgical experiences augment the community's eucharistic life. Chief among them are celebrations of reconciliation, anointing of the sick, and rites related to the initiation of new members. By their very nature each of these celebrations is an expression of the true nature of the local community and helps the community to express and thereby to deepen its experience of itself as a healing, caring, welcoming community continuing the life and ministry of the Lord Jesus.

For these blessings of participation, ministry, and variety, and for all the liturgical blessings of these decades too numerous to mention, we give thanks.

Acclamation

Who can remain silent when God's blessings are recounted? In the Eucharistic Prayer we join our voices with those of all the heavenly choir in a burst of praise as we acclaim, Holy, Holy, Holy.

Similarly, in face of God's constancy and goodness to us during these years of liturgical renewal, we shout out our praise that we are Church, that the liturgy is *ours*, that from age to age and most particularly in our own day God continues to gather us so that from east to west we might offer a perfect sacrifice of praise.

Epiclesis

A perfect sacrifice . . . ? Yes, because it is the sacrifice of the Lord which we offer to the Father. Yet even as we say those words we realize that we must call on God's power of transformation. The epiclesis is that moment of our prayer of praise and thanksgiving when we invoke the power of the Spirit to transform our gifts and to transform ourselves.

It is this very experience of "transformation" that the renewed liturgy urges upon us, in word and gesture, in feast and season, in sacrament and in symbol. Conversion is a word and a way of life writ large in the renewed rites of the community. Certainly one of the main reasons why the Council mandated the simplification of the rites was that they might be experienced as an invitation to the community to enter once again and more deeply into the Paschal Mystery of the Lord Jesus.

Conversion takes time. The seasons have been so designed that they open us in a cyclic way to new modes and depths of conversion. The recovery of rites of the catechumenate may be the single most significant factor in the liturgical renewal. If taken seriously these rites have the potential for transforming the Church, for the cate-chumenate presupposes that potential members are initiated into a community in the midst of the faithful who will walk with them, who will renew their own conversion, who will deepen their own appreciation of the paschal Mystery of Jesus' death and rising in their personal lives, and who will, by word, example, and most especially by their way of life, lead new members to hear and obey the Spirit more generously. A community cannot be unaffected by the presence of potential members. Their journey in our midst awakens in us the desire and the need to live in fact what we proclaim in word as our way of life.

Understood as celebrations of cross-road moments, as conversion moments in the lives of individuals, all of the sacraments have this unique potential for inviting conversion and transformation into Christ. The presumption must gain sway that we not celebrate sacraments prematurely. We must allow the Rite of Christian Initiation of Adults, its process and its methodology, to infuse our understanding and celebration of all the other sacramental passages. In each sacrament we must find ourselves engaged in process, supported and sustained in the midst of a community whose members are all on a journey of conversion into Christ.

"Epiclesis" is simply another way of saying that our transformation into Christ, begun at baptism, remains incomplete. Epiclesis is our way of acknowledging our utter dependence on the power of God's Spirit in the work of renewal.

Narrative of Institution

At each Eucharist we repeat the story of the final supper of the Lord with His disciples. We tell that story because it is *our* story and *our* mandate, the heart and center of our individual stories, the "glue" of our ecclesial lives. Caught suspended over the chasm between the "is" and the "ought," between what God has already done and what we still lack, we tell the story of Jesus' crossing over through death to life. We tell the story lest we lose heart.

Similarly, lest we get discouraged with the progress of the renewal, lest we wonder why that transformation seems always beyond our reach, we need to engage in another kind of story-telling and place this renewal in a larger perspective. The Council promulgated the Constitution on the Sacred Liturgy on December 4, 1963. Its implementation was left to a post-conciliar concilium of scholars and pastors from all over the world whose first task was to examine all of the rites of the community and to revise them in light of the community's tradition, its history, its layered theology, its pastoral adaptations over time. Note the commission was to revise ALL of the community's rites and ceremonies. It was a procedure established to guarantee that sound tradition and legitimate progress would be wedded in the renewal and that new forms of worship adopted for the community would grow organically from those already part of its rich treasury.

Now, one might say that this first phase of the renewal is almost finished. The monumental work of revising the Church's liturgical library nears completion and is, in fact, virtually achieved with the exception of a Book of Blessings and one or two other lesser books. In quite rapid succession the Revised Roman Missal, the Lectionary, the Orders of Marriage and Funerals, the rites of Pastoral Care of the Sick and the Rite of Reconciliation were released in Latin and translated into the vernacular. Within ten years a new liturgical library has filled our shelves. It is important to keep this fact in mind, to remember that we have only been praying in English for about a dozen years; for only a little more than a decade have we had access to rites revised to express more clearly that which they signify. This has been quite an achievement in such a short time. But many in our younger generations, even now those whom I teach in a graduate school of theology, have no active memory of what liturgy was like "before the Council," and often wonder why people continually refer to the Council as such a watershed. Soon we will have whole communities of worshippers who take for granted that which was such an incredible innovation in the life of the Church.

But what of the other part of the story, the reception of this library on the part of local churches? If studies on the changing attitudes of American Catholics toward the liturgy such as that conducted by the National Opinion Research Center at the request of the Federation of Diocesan Liturgical Commissions are fairly accurate in their analysis, it would appear that over eighty per cent of American Catholics supported the major reforms of Vatican II. Only in two areas was there real dissatisfaction, the loss of devotions and lay ministers of communion. Now that the former are being restored in a new mode and the latter are being accepted and welcomed in most communities, one might guess that dissatisfaction has ebbed to a very small minority. (It is important to note in passing that this minority, while minuscule in face of 55 million American Catholics touched and transformed by the renewal, is both well financed and extremely vocal. It is hoped that money and decibels will not mislead commentators on the American scene.)

In reporting on the state of liturgical renewal in the

American Church in the fall of 1984 to the Congress of Presidents and Secretaries of National Liturgical Commissions, Bishop John Cummins of Oakland, chairman of the Bishops' Committee on the Liturgy of the United States, concluded his remarks with the following positive summary:

> We present this report filled with experience of a quality of worship over these past years that has been perceptibly nourishing of faith. We note and we commend the energy that parishes and dioceses are exerting with consistency in the life of the church. We believe that worship has moved us to a new depth of prayer that is rich and vibrant.
>
> (*Origins* 14:25, December 6, 1984, 405.)

That, finally, is what the larger story of the renewal tells us. Twenty years later we enjoy a depth of liturgical prayer that is rich and vibrant and life-sustaining. Caught up in the immediate struggle of each change as it came along, we often saw it too narrowly as an issue of the survival or death of external liturgical forms inherited from our immediate ancestors in faith. Letting go and dying have been part of each experience of renewal. Yet we have also found new life in that dying. We have discovered a deeper continuity with the Church's long and rich tradition of worship and we have allowed that tradition to become a wellspring of new life and vitality. What the larger story of liturgical renewal is finally about is simply this: like those who have gone before us in faith, we in our day continue to "do this in memory of Him."

Anamnesis

Following the narrative of institution and consecration, the eucharistic prayer contains a brief summary statement through which the community calls to mind ("anamnesis" means remembrance) the highlights of the Paschal Mystery, the passion, resurrection and ascension of the Lord.

Having told our story of these last decades of renewal we now simply "make memorial" of the highlights of our liturgical journey: the early explosion of joy, the frequent hesitancy, the confusion, the sufferings, the reluctance, the misunderstanding which these years of renewal engendered. Most of all we remember that this renewal has not been an end in itself but has been only a means, but in fact the *best* means that the Fathers of the Second Vatican Council could think of, to recreate the *plebs sancta dei*, the holy people of God.

Offering

Having made the memorial of the Lord in its eucharistic prayer, the community here and now assembled offers Christ to the Father in the Holy Spirit. It is the Church's intention, according to the *General Instruction on the Roman Missal* that the community offers not only Christ, but gradually, daily, that we learn to offer ourselves and to be drawn into more perfect union with God and with one another.

It is perhaps this element of "offering" which serves to highlight one of the most prominent concerns of the renewal of the liturgy if we are to worship in spirit and in truth, and that is the way the liturgy is helping us to focus

on the relationship of liturgy and life experience. "Daily
we learn to offer ourselves." How many of us need to
reflect often on the relation of liturgy and life experience,
to raise the question for ourselves about how the liturgy is
a celebration of what is already going on in our lives, not a
creation of experience which does not exist. How many
of the country's best liturgists have lately turned to the
topic of the relationship of liturgy and social justice,
pondering the fact that a fully renewed liturgy does not
necessarily create a fully renewed community in deeper
union with God and one another.

How many are now raising questions about the depth of
the renewal since we do not seem to be appreciably more
just, more loving, more open to others, more ready to
open our hearts to a recent bumper sticker which seems to
express something of the irony of a renewal of liturgy
without concomitant renewal of life: If you love Jesus,
work for justice; any fool can honk.

Perhaps we have not pondered sufficiently the call to
participation as a mandate for *internal* as well as an
external worship. Perhaps we need to reflect on the
meaning of our "Amens," whether said with vigor or
indifference in expressing a commitment to a way of life.
Amen means "yes, I accept," "yes, I believe," "Yes, I will
act, with God's grace." Amen ratifies a way of life, of
completing Christ's work on earth, of proclaiming the
good news of salvation to the poor, freedom to prisoners,
joy to those in sorrow — all because we long to live and
pray to live "no longer for ourselves but for God." Amen
affirms the offering we wish to make by the grace of God,
the offering of ourselves with Christ and the Church.
Amen.

Intercessions

Having given praise and thanks to God, having recalled God's constancy and fidelity on our behalf, having recounted the extraordinary gifts God continues to lavish upon us, especially the grace of desire to offer ourselves that our Amen might be true—in the midst of such lavish praise and thanks, the community becomes once again beggar before God. Such is typical of Christian prayer. The intercessions are the community's moment to acknowledge its need of God and God's grace in order to participate in the building up of the kingdom and the completion of Christ's work on earth.

Reflecting on the progress of the liturgical renewal, our wish list might be long indeed, for while we have made great strides and remarkable achievements in these past two decades of liturgical reform, there are still so many areas where we have hardly begun. It is true that we have a new liturgical library. But the completion of the library was only the first stage of a reform to make the rites on the printed page come alive, to make the attitudes enfleshed in the rites touch our hearts.

So we take a moment to intercede for the continued renewal of the liturgy: We pray that true inculturation will take place across our country and our world. We pray that the community will be able to help shape the celebration of its own particular life, its experience, its needs, the genius of its various races and peoples, the language which unites it, the life experience which it comes together to celebrate in liturgy.

We pray that the gifts of women will be accepted and blessed in liturgical celebrations, that their particular experience will be recognized and welcomed through the use of inclusive language, that their particular gifts of intuition and compassion might somehow help to shape penitential practice, that their insights into the Word of God might be heard in our Churches, that their gifts for service at the altar and for proclamation might be honored and publicly blessed, that those women who are "strong, loving and wise" among us might be chosen to preside at the community's prayer and included in all facets of the Church's ministry and life.

We pray that the homily, that "necessary source of nourishment of the Christian life" will come alive in our day, that homilists will prepare carefully and well, reflecting both on the Word of God and on the life experience of the community, placing the two in dialogue that a new life-giving and life-sustaining word might be born. We pray that the community will demand such preaching of its leaders and take whatever steps are necessary to educate all of us about the vital role of the Word of God and its interpretation in our lives.

Even as the texts of all the rites are revised and even as we care to make our language truly inclusive of all members of the worshipping community, we pray that we will be able to admit our excessive wordiness and our propensity to talk symbols to death. And we pray that having admitted this, we may come to understand how to praise God with bodily attitude and silence as well as with voice and sound.

We pray that our liturgies will reflect what is happening not just in our communities but in our late twentieth century world as well, that they will recognize the perils of nuclear war, the economic injustices of our system, and the whole range of issues which touch our reverence for human life. We hope and we pray that our liturgies will not be disconnected from real life experience but will immerse us in that real world and will commission us to activity on behalf of the kingdom.

We pray, as well, that we not become faint-hearted, "we" here in the American Church or "we" in Rome, that we will boldly continue to allow the vision of Vatican II to inform our liturgical theology and its celebration, that we not back down in renewing our community, yielding to those who would reverse the trends of Vatican II. We pray that we will recognize that attitude for what it is, namely, a challenge to the ecclesiology of the Council and to the collegiality of those Bishops who are attempting to implement the Council with courage and imagination.

We pray that our sacraments will be rooted in life experience and thus true symbols of our way of life; that anointing will be symbol of a community of care, communal reconciliation symbol of a community in need of reconciliation and healing, initiation symbol of a community eager to join new members to its way of life and willing to pay the price of fidelity to that way, and finally, eucharist as true food for the journey symbolizing a community committed to its pilgrimage in faith.

We pray that the eucharist will be our authentic response to the God who breaks into our ordinary time with extraordinary grace and invites us to participate in the death and rising of Jesus for the life of the world. We pray that the eucharist will reveal to us that we are sinners and at one and the same time loved by God and liberated for God's service. We pray that the eucharist will draw us continually to ever-deeper union with God and to a new future.

Doxology

At the end of our prayer of praise and thanksgiving for the mighty acts of God in Jesus and the truly remarkable acts of God in the liturgical renewal of the American Church, we can only pause to add a final burst of praise. Perhaps it would be appropriate to praise God not simply despite the tensions and the contradictions of our renewal and our life, but because of them.

Let us praise God who has counted us worthy to stand in His presence and to serve him. Let us praise God who has given us a sense of the long journey still ahead of us and the tensions and differences of the moment — recognizing that all of this is a sign of life and of love for worship as a way of life and an expression of the community we are called to become.

There are several wonderful lines in Preface IV for weekdays which gather up our praise and thanks, gather up also our story and our remembering, our offering and intercession, and place the whole of our eucharist in the appropriate context:

> All powerful and ever-living God,
> we do well always and everywhere to give you
> thanks.
> You have no need of our praise,
> yet our desire to thank you is itself your gift.
> Our prayer of thanksgiving adds nothing to your
> greatness,
> but makes us grow in your grace.

This weekday preface may be source of consolation and courage for our community of the American Church. God does not need our eucharist, God does not need our praise and our thanksgiving, yet it is God who has placed in our hearts the desire to make eucharist, it is God's initiative which draws out our response. If that is so, we may only conclude that the God who has brought us thus far on our liturgical journey will remain faithful and will complete the work which is so well begun in us.

> Through him,
> with him,
> in him,
> in the unity of the Holy Spirit,
> all glory and honor is yours,
> almighty Father,
> for ever and ever.
> Amen.

Merton, Spiritual Guide for the '80s

M. Basil Pennington, O.C.S.O.

When I think of Philip Scharper, I think of a man who made a difference, a man who had a distinctive impact on American Catholicism as it has progressed through the second half of the twentieth century. Both through his own writings and through the writings of the many others whom he supported and brought to positions of influence as an editor, Scharper has spoken creatively and challengingly to our generation. Under his leadership the daring Orbis Books has remained effectively at the cutting edge of American Catholicism in its global concern and action.

And if I go on to think of other men of such quality and impact, the next name that comes to my mind is that of my brother Cistercian, Thomas Merton. It is more than a decade since Merton completed his pilgrimage among us, yet his influence goes on unabated. His early books remain the best-sellers of Catholic publishing, read by Catholics and non-Catholics alike. Each year more of his unpublished legacy comes to stand at their side, while biographies of him reach the best-seller lists. And all of this is finding its way into print in many languages. Not only is Merton the one Western spiritual writer read by the monks of Mount Athos — and they are clamoring for more of him to be translated into Greek — but he is the inspiration of the most effective peace movement in Italy and read with respect by men and women working for justice and peace in such diverse places as Tokyo and Johannesburg. Ever since the publication of his autobiography in 1948 — a book that has appeared in at least a half dozen major languages — Merton has had a widespread appeal. And this did not lessen as he turned his attention more and more to social and political issues which had a particular relevance to his adopted country. For he saw things more and more clearly in the context of an absolutely basic and integral humanism. In the end that is not only what creation and re-creation, redemption and sanctification are all about, it is what speaks to the deepest heart of every human and calls it forth.

Recently a book of essays on Thomas Merton was published with the title: *Getting It All Together*. The title aptly expresses the essence of the spirituality that Merton lived and offers to us through his many books and articles.

Thomas Merton, known in the monastic world as Father M. Louis, O.C.S.O., was a Cistercian for more than half of his uniquely full and fruitful life. The Cistercians have been popularly called Trappists, a named that comes from their first days in America after the French Revolution. The first monks to come to America came from the Abbey of La Grande Trappe. The name Trappist became legendary, synonymous with silence, penance and austerity. One went to the Trappists to die — however long it might take.

But the monks see it differently (and thanks largely to Merton most others now also do). The Cistercians look to the magnificent heritage that comes to them from the great Christian humanists of the twelfth century: Bernard of Clairvaux, Aelred of Rievaulx, William of Saint Thierry and others. With the genius that was his, and the insight, Merton as a novice in Gethsemani Abbey in 1941-44 devoured the writings of these holy forebears, realized he shared their charism, and set about seeking to assimilate their wisdom and live it to the full. If he was in the end a realized man — and he was — it was because he realized the potential of who he was: a Christian monk with the Cistercian charism.

Not everyone perhaps would be ready to recognize Merton as a realized man or, as Catholics might say, a canonizable saint. He doesn't fit some of our more conventional pictures of the 'holy monk'. To find him, just a couple of weeks before his death, spending his evenings in the bars of Colombo and staying at the most deluxe hotel in a city plagued by much dehumanizing poverty is a cause of great scandal for some. Others are more scandalized to find this Catholic monk taking off his shoes and going barefoot and reverent in a Buddhist sanctuary and, even more scandalous, experiencing God there in a most profound way.

Yet those freer from preconceptions, more open to the reality of the man, did not hesitate to proclaim what they experienced. Dr. Koko Soedjatmoko, the Indonesian Ambassador to the United States, who spent a day with Merton about three months before his death, made this remarkable statement:

> If there is one impression that has stayed with me all along
> it is a memory of one of the very few people I have known in
> this world with an inner freedom which is almost total. It
> was, I felt, an inner freedom which was not negative, in
> terms of something else, but it was like water that constantly
> flows out of a well.

A person much closer to Merton, a disciple who became his father, Abbot Flavian Burns, said: "Thomas Merton was for me a spiritual master, and I would say he is the most extraordinary spiritual master that I've met, a living master. ...I think he was a saint."

Michael Mott in his 'authorized' biography of Merton reports that to almost all he met in Asia, even in brief encounters, Merton was "a living example of the freedom and transformation of consciousness which meditation can give."

Merton speaks powerfully to us in the '80s. That he does so is attested by many facts. The sale of Merton's books, almost all still readily available in paperback twenty, thirty, and forty years after their publication, goes on unabated. It would be hard to count the number of centers around the country which now bear the name of Merton, and the many conferences that are regularly being held in his memory or to study his heritage. Colleges across the nation offer courses about Merton and his literary and social contribution. And the list of doctoral and master's theses about him keeps growing. Merton speaks powerfully to us in these '80s precisely because he did 'get it all together' — he was an integrated person, a Christian humanist, a Cistercian, in the best sense of the name.

Ours is a humanistic age. One is tempted to say, excessively so. But that is not quite accurate. While it is true that there is an exaggerated value placed on some dimensions of human life, the unfortunate truth is that man for who he truly is, is not appreciated adequately. Our age has discovered, or rather rediscovered the value of some of the dimensions of human life which the Church and society as a whole had not respected or valued in recent centuries. In cultivating and enjoying these values other truly basic human values have sometimes been left behind with sad consequences and even with dehumanizing aberrations. Even where this has not been the case, where we have become more human, more in touch with the aspirations of the human mind and heart, there has been a growing sense of a need for something more. To attain that something more is it necessary to turn our backs on what we have found? Can the experience of the goods of human life which we have discovered and want to continue to experience be a part of our lives even while we reach for and enjoy the transcendent, for that something beyond what we need? Is a renunciation of the good things of this world the only route? Do we all have to become monks? Do monks themselves have to turn their backs on good human experiences in order to be true to their quest, to their vocation?

Merton's answer is 'no.'

Merton shows us that holiness, wholeness, the fullness of life is to be found in integration, in true humanness, in a centered life, a grounded life. We do not want to go back to the dichotomies of the not so distant past. We want to keep our gains in human consciousness, purify them, and integrate them into the richness of our religious heritages, coming to a new fullness of life, one more truly satisfying and worthy of who we really are as human persons, images of God called to full likeness. Merton did not come to the realization of this easily. And his life to the end was something of a struggle to arrive at and preserve the freedom to live it.

Merton's life can be summed up, I believe, as a quest for life, for freedom, for the freedom to live life to the full. His younger years were marked by an excessive false humanism expressing itself in many aberrant ways, even while he explored greater causes in response to a largely unconscious yearning within him for something more worthy of who he was. When finally, with the help of friends and readings and God's grace, he did find that something more, or the way to seek it, he reacted to the aberrations of his earlier days and to all that was associated with them, to the 'world'. He fled to Gethsemani and was glad to hear the great doors of the monastery close firmly behind him. Unfortunately — though really fortunately, he couldn't leave it all outside. A very significant part of that 'world' came in with him — himself, with all his human gifts and qualities. Merton was well aware of this crack in the door — a rather significant one — and for years he tried to stuff it with resolutions and obediences.

Thomas Merton was blessed with a very wise old spiritual father when he first came to Gethsemani. Dom Frederic Dunne understood that our attitudes toward the goods of creation, even those goods which are given to us most personally as our own qualities of soul and mind, do have to be purified. We do need to find freedom so that we can use these goods as we truly want, to attain the end we want and to enjoy them to the full. We don't ordinarily find this by repression or denial, but by struggle and assimilation.

Dom Frederic put Father Louis to writing; then to writing about himself. He had to look at his life and the 'world' again, in some way hold it again for a re-evaluation. Then the young monk was put to teaching. His courses included the Greek Fathers. There is no better way to learn something than to teach it. Merton learned from these Fathers that between the *bios prakticos*, the practical life, the life of the world that Merton so wanted to leave behind, and *theoria*, the contemplation of divine things, toward which the young monk aspired, there is the *theoria praktice*, the perception of the presence of the divine in the created, in the world. The *logoi*, the seminal creative expression of God, God himself as creating, and the manifest imaging of his being and beauty, reside in every created thing and above all in every human person.

Merton assimilated this well — intellectually. His lectures set it forth clearly for his students. But before it could become a transforming realization in his own life something deeper had to take place. And it did. Merton, by and large, was quite a private person. Even though he was an inveterate keeper of journals, until the last years when love gave him a new freedom he was quite guarded in these, and certainly so when he edited them for publication. It is in his letters we get some of the most candid and insightful glimpses of what was going on within. The experience that Merton had on the corner of Fourth and Walnut on March 18, 1958 is well known from his writings and the many commentaries on it. What has not been so well known is its Jungian background revealed by Merton in an exceptionally candid letter to an extraordinary friend, Boris Pasternak. It is worth quoting at length:

> It is a simple enough story but obviously I do not tell it to people — you are the fourth who knows it, and there seems to be no point in a false discreteness that might restrain me

from telling you since it is clear that we have so very much in common.

One night I dreamt that I was sitting with a very young Jewish girl of fourteen or fifteen, and that she suddenly manifested a very deep and pure affection for me and embraced me so that I was moved to the depths of my soul. I learned that her name was "Proverb," which I thought very simple and beautiful. And also I thought: "She is of the race of Saint Anne." I spoke to her of her name, and she did not seem to be proud of it, because it seemed that the other girls mocked her for it. But I told her that it was a very beautiful name, and there the dream ended. A few days later when I happened to be in a nearby city, which is very rare for us, I was walking alone in the crowded street and suddenly saw that everybody was Proverb and that in all of them shone her extraordinary beauty and purity and shyness, even though they did not know who they were and were perhaps ashamed of their names — because they were mocked on account of them. And they did not know their real identity as the Child so dear to God who, from before the beginning, was playing in His sight all days, playing in the world.

By this experience, Merton came to know not just intellectually but experientially the goodness and the beauty of all God's creatures, the presence of God in them. Merton spoke of this experience "as if waking from a dream" — "Yesterday, in Louisville, at the corner of 4th and Walnut, suddenly I realized that I loved all the people and that none of them were, or could be, totally alien to me." It was one of the great moments in his steady course toward what he would call in an article published shortly before his death, "final integration."

Another characteristic of the '80s has been 'roots.' Haley's stirring search, shared by unprecedented millions on television, spoke to a rootless people. The attraction of many of the masters from Asia has been that they are well rooted. They speak out of an ancient, powerful, and living tradition. That attraction has now waned because their roots are not our roots. Merton's spirituality of integration is especially attractive to the '80s in America because it is well rooted and the tradition it is rooted in is our tradition. Cistercian spirituality as it blossomed forth in the twelfth century was one of the most complete and beautiful expressions of Christian tradition. In Merton it went on to integrate the richness of the later centuries, of Eastern and Western Christendom, of all the spiritual forces that have created our heritage.

Tradition, living tradition, is a constantly growing, self-enriching reality. *Tra-ditio*, it is a handing on. But each of us recipients is to receive it fully into ourselves and allow it to come alive in us. Merton, in his earliest days at Gethsemani, sought to receive fully and to possess the Cistercian heritage. And he went on from there. In the spirit of the Cistercian Fathers of the twelfth century who brought together the heritage of Antioch and Alexandria, of Christianity East and West, of incarnationalism and transcendence, Merton sought to integrate the spiritual riches of the ensuing centuries. In 1957 he wrote: "If I can unite *in myself*, in my own spiritual life, the thought in the East and the West, of the Greek and Latin Fathers. . . ." Not many Catholics were thinking in that way in those pre-Vatican II days. When he reported this in *Conjectures of a Guilty Bystander* in 1965 he added "the Russian with the Spanish mystics."

Merton did not need the encouragement given by the Second Vatican Council to begin reaching yet further. His early life prepared him for it — his travels with a father who came from the other side of the world and down under, his readings, and his friends. Merton was a global man, a cosmic person. As long as he lived he reached and he reached, to other classes, to other races, to other creeds, to other nations, and to other cultures. It would lead him to die in far away Bangkok, on a journey with ever widening horizons.

With the world becoming a global village, we of the '80s are more and more conscious of the one human family. We want to be fully a part of it, embracing the values as well as the cares and concerns of each and all. Merton gives us a context for doing this.

The word 'cosmic' might well have the same derivative meaning as 'global' but it has a very different connotation. It is much fuller than global. It is the context within which we can truly embrace the global and make it our own, integrating it with all its human, political, social, economic and religious concerns. The deepest aspirations of the human spirit are more than global. They are infinite. We desire not only to know all, to be in touch with all that is going on (Merton had an amazing, insightful knowledge of 'what was going on', amazing for any man but especially for an enclosed monk — perhaps this highlights the role of the monk and the truth that one needs to get apart to see, to get true perspective), we want to care, to embrace all in love. And do this without being burnt out or washed up. We can do it if we are grounded in the source of all love, Infinite Love. If we know we are so grounded and know how to draw on this, how to come from this, be one with this, then we will know how to love, embracing all, one with the Infinite Love, who is God. This Merton clearly taught us; in his life and in his writings he has showed us how.

At the very heart and center of all that Merton was, said and did was his life of prayer. His was a very simple way of prayer — again, something that appeals to us in the '80s and responds to our needs.

In a letter to a Sufi scholar, Aziz Ch. Abdul, Merton speaks most openly about his own prayer:

> Now you ask about my method of meditation. Strictly speaking I have a very simple way of prayer. It is centered entirely on attention to the presence of God and to His will and His love. That is to say that it is centered on *faith* by which alone we can know the presence of God. One might say this gives my meditation the character described by the Prophet as "being before God as if you saw Him." Yet it does not mean imagining anything or conceiving a precise image of God, for to my mind this would be a kind of idolatry. On the contrary, it is a matter of adoring Him as all. . . . There is in my heart this great thirst to recognize totally the nothingness of all that is not God. My prayer is then a kind of praise rising up out of the center of Nothingness and Silence. If I am still present "myself" this I recognize as an obstacle. If He wills he can then make the nothingness into a total clarity. If He does not will, then the Nothingness actually seems to itself to be an object and remains an obstacle. Such is my ordinary way of prayer, or meditation. It is not "thinking about" anything, but a direct seeking of the Face of the Invisible. Which cannot be found unless we become lost in Him who is Invisible.

This is the prayer which has become known popularly as 'centering prayer.'

In his more formal writings Merton spoke of it this way:

> Unless we discover this deep self, which is hidden with Christ in God, we will never really know ourselves as persons. Nor will we know God. For it is by the door of this deep self that we enter into the spiritual knowledge of God.

(And indeed, if we seek our true selves it is not in order to contemplate ourselves but to pass beyond ourselves and find Him.)

The fact is, however, that as you descend into the depths of your own spirit . . . and arrive somewhere near the center of what you are, you are confronted with the inescapable truth that, at the very root of your existence you are in constant and immediate and inescapable contact with the infinite power of God.

A man cannot enter into the deepest center of himself and pass through the center into God unless he is able to pass entirely out of himself and empty himself and give himself to other people in the purity of a selfless love.

In his last days in the United States Merton gathered with special friends at Redwoods Abbey. The sharing was rich and deep. He left these final words about personal prayer, truly practical advice:

It's a risky thing to pray, and the danger is that our very prayers get between God and us. The great thing is not to pray, but to go directly to God. If saying your prayers is an obstacle to prayer, cut it out. Let Jesus pray. Thank God Jesus is praying. Forget yourself. Enter into the prayer of Jesus. Let him pray in you. . . . the best way to pray is: stop. Let prayer pray within you, whether you know it or nor.

Merton knew what a struggle it takes to be a man of prayer, a man of peace, in the midst of the shattering concerns of our times. He never gave up the struggle. Prayer remained the focus and source of his life. As it must be for the man or woman who hopes to negotiate the '80s not only successfully, but in a way that truly makes a difference.

It was the great mosaic icons that first awakened Merton's faith in Rome. The icon of the Cosmic Christ in the all-embracing 'icon' of the Byzantine church, an icon of the embrace of society, world and all creation, is a reality that powerfully 'iconifies,' expresses in classical hieratic form the ultimate stance of Merton — if we soften the classically severe features of the Pantocrator with the Oriental smile of the Buddha. Merton had a way of not taking himself too seriously! And that, too, makes him such an eminently attractive 'saint' for the '80s.

Catholic Higher Education
A Personal Reflection

Theodore M. Hesburgh, C.S.C.

Catholic higher education underwent significant change in the lifetime of Philip Scharper. Rather than try to treat that vast topic in limited space, let me illustrate what has happened by focusing on the institution I know best—the University of Notre Dame, where I have been a student, teacher and administrator for more than a half-century. The developments of which I write could be found in the lives of similar schools, such as Georgetown, Boston College, Villanova or the Loyolas, but, again, one speaks best of what one knows best.

Notre Dame was a good university in its genre when I first knew it. It is a far better and quite different institution today after a half-century of development following almost a century of earlier history, beginning with a log cabin in northern Indiana where the founder, Father Edward Sorin, with total assets of about $300.00 declared it the University of Notre Dame du Lac. A century later it was still in essence a college, but on the verge of becoming, at long last, a university.

The post-World War II years were exciting and productive for all of higher education, including Catholic. Notre Dame's student body rose from about 3,000 prewar to just under 10,000 today, most of whom live on campus. Students of ever-increasing academic qualifications came from every state in the Union and sixty-six foreign countries. One of them, Jose Napoleon Duarte, is President of El Salvador today. Another, Gu Yijian, is Secretary General of the Chinese Academy of Sciences. At home, four have been state governors, a dozen are or have been U. S. congressmen, over thirty are college presidents today, more than three thousand alumni and alumnae are engaged in higher education. Over eight hundred are presidents or vice presidents of corporations. There are admirals, generals, and astronauts who are alumni. Thousands are medical doctors, lawyers, judges. Dozens are bishops and hundreds are priests. There are poets, artists, actors, authors, and journalists of national repute. One would hope there have been some saints, too, certainly a few martyrs.

The institution itself has undergone a formidable development in the last half century. The annual budget has risen from a million dollars to over one hundred and sixty million annually. Faculty salaries and benefits have risen from the bottom to the highest category in the nation. Externally sponsored research has come from almost none to about fifteen million dollars annually. Student scholarship aid rose from a few thousand to thirty-eight million dollars this year, affecting sixty-four per cent of the student body. Our ninth Rhodes Scholar leaves for Oxford this year. About 250 doctorates were awarded last year in over twenty disciplines and hundreds of master's degrees in over forty subjects. Library holdings went from two hundred thousand to more than a million and a half.

During this time, the physical facilities of the University were doubled to more than a hundred buildings at a cost of more than two hundred million dollars. The University is practically debt-free. The endowment has grown from three million to two hundred and seventy-five million, the twenty-first largest endowment among all the private universities in the land. From none, there are now over forty distinguished professorships endowed at more than a million dollars apiece. Twenty-five more are partially endowed, with another thirty or more expected in the near future.

Computing facilities now cost as much as the library, a development unknown thirty years ago. There are two national research facilities on the campus, one in radiation chemistry and another in germfree life. Microfilm collections in Medieval Studies include the whole Ambrosian Collection from Milan, comprising over ten thousand priceless manuscripts and art works, parts of which are now touring America. The Snite Museum has one of the finest art collections among American universities. The University Press — of special interest to Philip Scharper — is the largest at any Catholic university and has published hundreds of outstanding books, especially in philosophy and theology.

Notre Dame has student branches in London, England; in Angers, France; in Innsbruck, Austria; in Rome, Italy; in Mexico City; in Tokyo, Japan, and Tienjin, China. There will shortly be others in Jerusalem and Cairo.

To this *tour d'horizon* of quantifiable progress must be added some organizational changes that have had profound effects on the life and spirit of the University.

Following Vatican Council II, in which it was proclaimed that laymen and laywomen in the Church should be given responsibilities commensurate with their competence and dedication, the University which, like so many others, was owned and operated by the founding religious order, the Congregation of Holy Cross, was completely handed over to a largely lay Board of Trustees (42 laymen and laywomen, 8 Holy Cross priests) under a lay Chairman.

This was the largest religious organization in the world to be passed over to lay control, and one of the first. At the time, 1967, many said, "There goes the Catholic character of the University, just as happened to most of the Protestant-founded universities in America." In fact, such doubters were wrong.

The first act of the lay trustees was to specify for the first time in a new set of University Statutes and By-Laws (we operate under a charter granted by the legislature of the State of Indians, 1844, in which religion is not mentioned) that Notre Dame is, and will remain in perpetuity, a Catholic university, with the founding religious congregation serving as administrators and faculty members as qualified and, especially, serving the pastoral needs of the University.

The religious are now for the first time paid the same salaries as laymen. From these funds, the expenses of the religious are paid, and all the rest of this income is rebated to the University, making Holy Cross one of the largest benefactors of the University, contributing over recent years more than ten million dollars.

One of the first questions posed by the new lay Board was "What in fact is a Catholic university and what are you doing to assure that you are such?" Two or three years later, the administration and faculty published the COUP Report (Committee on University Priorities). In essence, the first priority is the Catholic character of the University, with all the others bearing on what makes for academic excellence in such a Catholic university as Notre Dame.

The Trustees then asked for price tags to be put on these priorities. The amount of $130 million was the price. A Campaign for Notre Dame was mounted. Five years later, we had raised $180 million. Then followed the PACE Report (Priorities and Commitment to Excellence). Again, the new priorities were priced, this time totaling $300 million. Thus a new campaign is being mounted and should be completed successfully by the end of the eighties.

The lay Board also decided early in its life (one of its first official acts) that the academic administration of the University should be conducted by the administration and faculty, according to Articles of Administration drawn up by them, reviewed every ten years, and approved by the Trustees. This is somewhat unusual in university-Trustee relationships, but has served us well and avoided many tensions that exist elsewhere.

The Trustees constantly review the process, but have never failed to approve any new legislation of the Academic Council, comprised of faculty (majority), administrators, and students. There has been a healthy balance between basic policy which the Trustees ultimately decide and the administration of policy which is left to University personnel.

Since the Trustees appoint all of the officers of the University and review their performance each year, there is a good balance and control. The Trustees are also a firm buffer against any undue pressure on the University from outside authorities of State or Church. Legitimate autonomy and freedom in the University is guaranteed by this arrangement. So far, the Chairman and the President have closely collaborated and have respected each other's role and responsibility.

The new administrative role by a largely lay Board has made for a much stronger institution with ever more clearly stated goals, together with strong commitment to achieve them. Mutual support is the order of the day, and it does work for the common good and steady growth of the institution, even and especially as regards its Catholic character.

This is a new pattern of organization for a Catholic university, and it does work, in my judgment, much better than the old. I have not had five minutes of trouble with the Trustees. Their role has been very supportive, but then, we have been very fortunate thus far by having had highly intelligent and very competent Chairmen who really understand what a true Catholic university can and should be. We have also had as many as 18 Trustees with earned doctorates and several who are or have been university and college presidents. The new arrangement has likewise been good for the religious community whose role now is not simply to own and operate, but to serve without the temptations of ownership. There is also more satisfaction for religious in knowing that they hold their positions not because they are members of the Congregation, but because they are judged competent to perform the tasks to which they are nominated and for which they compete with others.

One of the other significant policies inaugurated by the Trustees was the decision in 1972 to change from a 130-

year old all-male institution to a coeducational university. There are now 2,600 women students and more than 100 women faculty members, and growing. This, too, reflects a new concern for the place of women in Catholic higher education and Catholic life in general.

Notre Dame is manifestly better for the new and vital presence of women faculty members and students. We were blessed for many years by the next-door presence of St. Mary's College for women. We did try to merge with them in 1970-72, but failing that, we find that coeducation at home and the continuing presence of more than 1,700 women students across the road is, in a way, the best of both worlds for both of us. We have many forms of educational and social collaboration. We have not sorted out all of our problems with coeducation, but I believe everyone has been surprised at how well it has worked and how much better off we all are because of this fundamental change.

A third development within Notre Dame has been a heightened sense of service. All universities should be of service to the local, national, and international communities within which they exist, but a Catholic university has a double duty beyond this. We have to serve the Church in the way that only universities can, to be a place in which the Church can do its thinking and research, and, beyond this, we must instill in our students a habit of serving the less fortunate as a very real expression of Catholic faith and life. I believe we are doing both of these special functions much better than ever before.

In the matter of serving the Church, we are one of three national centers for liturgical research, education, and practice. Incidentally, the liturgical life of the students is both enthusiastic and almost universally practiced. Worship and prayer are far ahead of national and, especially, international norms. The best Catholic university in Europe has only three per cent of its students regularly attending Mass and receiving the Sacraments. Our figure would be over ninety per cent, and it is matched by a practice of Christian concern and care of the less fortunate. About a third of our students are engaged weekly in various forms of service to the needy young and old in our community. About ten percent of our graduates volunteer a year or two of total Christian service to the unfortunate of this world, both here and abroad.

In other areas, we have made the most basic study of Catholic elementary and secondary education in the United States and are now engaged in the widest study of American parishes ever made. In both studies, costing over a half a million dollars each, we have had almost total support from the Catholic bishops. We have also collaborated in the recent Catholic Bishops' pastorals on nuclear war and on the American economy. We are engaged in continuing historical studies of American Catholicism, immigration and refugees, civil rights, and Third World development, especially in Latin America.

In conclusion, may I say that Catholic higher education is alive and well, growing in the excellence of its faculty and students, involved in a wide variety of basic Christian concerns, producing graduates who carry these concerns fruitfully, intelligently, and faithfully into their private, public, professional, and family lives. It is not a story of total success; no human endeavor, even with the help of divine grace, ever is. But the world and the Church would be much poorer today without the growing contribution of Catholic students, alumni and alumnae, and without the reality of Christian higher education, at Notre Dame and elsewhere.

The Signs of Peace

Daniel Berrigan, S.J.

About this time, Herod began to persecute certain ones of
the church... He proceeded to arrest Peter... He put him
in prison, delivering him to four squads of soldiers...So
Peter was kept in prison; but prayer for him was made
unremittingly by the church...

And on the very night when Herod was about to bring him
out, Peter was sleeping between two soldiers, bound with a
double chain; and guards were in front of the door.

And behold, an angel of the Lord suddenly appeared,.and a
light shone in the cell. The angel struck Peter's side, roused
him saying: Get up quickly. And the chains fell off his hands.

(Acts, c. 12)

Deliverance by the power of God, whether from
illness, travail, danger, accident, malice, and above all,
death — these are hard to give ear to, let alone belief.

The times are such that a far different voice than that of

Peter's angel whispers in our ear. It is a voice of judges, juntas, shahs, executioners, torturers, deceivers, prosecutors, and others of like mind and mindlessness. Prison is the order of the day, not the opening of gates. Torture and starvation and disappearance, rather than freedom, dignity, the dance of life. And death above all, beyond all, at the end of all; death the universal threat, the universal solvent, the darling of dictators and mad geneticists and abortionists and star warriors. The money is on death, death hedges no bets. It is life that is endangered and even despised, thrown away, pushed between the cracks of the great cities. Death in war, death equally in peace; or what passes for peace. But life worth living, life cherished, life given its chance, given place? how rarely!

Confronted with such a world, choices are made, leading in either of two directions. On the one hand, some choose not to see. Blunting of conscience occurs, consciences grow heedless and selfish. They achieve a kind of spurious normalcy, suffocating and single minded. Since the world is a mess, the reasoning goes, one had best rein in high resolve and broad ideals — for the duration.

Others look on the chaos of the world, are struck with horror, and shortly become sources of chaos. They plunge off in all directions, charging at windmills. Needless to say, they achieve nothing, or next to it. And finally, moral exhaustion overtakes them.

There must be a better way. In the midst of dead ends, moral detours, there must be a way of living humanly, of obeying one's faith, of remaining sensitive and firm, thoughtful and courageous, of healing and being healed; of standing somewhere, in the honored phrase.

I remember one sign of peace; a sign of peacemaking, more accurately. And a sign of deliverance as well.

In the summer of 1984, seven friends went on trial in Syracuse, New York. On a November morning of the year previous, they entered the guarded acres of Griffiss Air Force Base nearby, and proceeded to damage an enormous B-52 bomber, laying to with household hammers, marking the monster with their own blood, incapacitating its horrid threat of nuclear murder.

Practically everyone said in one way or another, that it couldn't be done. Most said it shouldn't be done. Many in fact shy away from even discussing such acts; they dread the thought of entering on such toilsome and perilous ground. A very welter of objections is raised like warriors springing from dragon's teeth. There are religious objections, practical objections, legal objections, esthetic objections. All unknowingly, some object from simple confusion, others from an overrefined conscience. Some wince because the tactic lies so close to the gospel bone; others because the tactic is not laid out biblically, jot and tittle. Still others declare that the whole mess of arms, arms makers, armories, arms researchers—this is beyond all rational control, anyone's control.

Some haul out alternatives; the dusty pieties of secular recourse. Isn't it best to stay within the law? Have you tried writing your president? Some point to blood obligations or property obligations or responsibilities; as though indeed, blood or conscience, and conscience or property, and each of these ikons were very images of God. Some had bought a farm, some traded in oxen, someone had taken a wife, another had to bury his fathers. And finally, there were those who confessed, ruefully and honorably, to dearth of courage.

Perhaps I can venture a moral profile of my seven friends. They lay no great claim to bravery; indeed, they confess to fear and trembling, to second, and even third thoughts; to a shaking hand as they grasp this fierce and harrowing sword, which they purpose somehow to transform into a plow.

Indeed, they tend to see themselves in those gospel stories wherein nobility or high resolve or holiness are celebrated — but off to one side, less noble side. They waver between what can be done and what should be done. They breathe meantime, almost with ecstasy, the spice of life, loving their spouses and friends as they do, begetting and raising children, in some cases seeing their children's children born in the world. They dread jail as a necessary evil, no less evil for being necessary; indeed, if anything, more evil for that. Finally, they are by no means detached from their good repute, which they regard, with Shakespeare as a peerless jewel.

To them also occur, in full force and logic and moral weight, the multiple objections stemming like very umbilicals, from community obligations, from professions, from vows and priesthood — perhaps most of all, from longed for normalcy. Yet they have cut the cord, and moved into the shadows.

Not, if I may speak for them, in any expectation of miracles. At least not in the spectacular sense, that judges will awaken to the dawn of truth, that icy prosecutors will melt under the sun of justice, that prison gates will spring. Such things may conceivably come to pass; in all likelihood they will not. And for sanity's sake, one had best proceed on the assumption that they will not.

What occurred during the trial went something like this. The seven were tried according to the rules of law; which is to say, a kind of straitjacket bound their free souls in the court room. A gag was placed on their tongues; not that they were forbidden to enter a broad defense, but the judge always claimed the last word; and his last word forbade the jury to take the defendants seriously. The defense based on conscience was forced to yield to points of law. It was a no win situation; they were allowed to talk at length of their love of children, their fears for the children's survival, their religious passion, their love of life and the God of life; but all these motives were finally excised by the blade of that sword named Justice. Thus amputated by the mad surgery of the system, our friends, bloody but unbowed, were, in the inelegant and telling phrase, disposed of.

Which is to say, they were convicted and sentenced in accord with laws designed to protect a public building against vandals, a home against armed robbery, flesh and bone against rapists and muggers. No miracles here, to be sure, but only 'justice.' In due course they were locked up, some for three years, some for two, under the assumption that rights of property and person are better served with such as they segregated from decent humans. Children now will be safer, intact, since the notorious Seven are behind bars.

My friends, in other words, despite all courage, altruism, outcry, are a long way from anything resembling miracles. They have not evoked a change of heart in officials or improved public understanding. The world goes on. Bombs and bombers and bombmakers prosper and multiply. Prosecutors continue to prosecute, judges to judge, juries to convict, marshals and guards to 'do their job.' And in the great world, at the far frontier of the empire, peasants disappear, torture grows more exquisite, the homeless beat at the walls in vain, presidents smile and beguile. My friends are a long way indeed from the springing of the prison gates. Our nuclear winter, a matter of degradation in nature and destruction of soul, proceeds; an arctic incursion indeed.

And yet, and yet. In so reflecting, I am leaving something out. I remind my soul; I am recounting only 'the facts.' I am writing like a court reporter, in the cockpit of event, mechanically tapping out a kind of shorthand; words, words, words. This is the world's news, laid before the world's eyes; the world as the world sees itself. And the news, given the world, is bad.

But this is not the way Christians are to read, or to write, the news. Especially not, as that news, its power and ploys, its revengeful blows, fall on them. Not through judge's eyes, or prosecutor eyes, or jury's eyes — or the president's eyes. Not through the media, not through the air force, not through General Electric, not through the pentagon. Not through jargon and incantation and calls to blood loyalty and rallying around the flag. Through none of these, we are told. Better, we are warned.

What then? Let us say for a start, we are to view 'the world, the way it goes,' through the eyes of Peter the prisoner, calmly sleeping the night away, 'When Herod was about to bring him out to the people' (a euphemism, indicating a public execution.) Are we to conclude that Peter slept on, indifferent toward his fate? or that he was merely stupefied with terror?

In either case, we had best attend, with the attention urged by desperate circumstance, to a single sentence of the episode. 'All the time Peter was under guard, earnest prayer was made for him to God by the church.'

Simply stated, we have here the absolute clash and conflict of oppositions, of powers and reliances, of practices common to church and state; all these, and an outcome. The prayer of the church prevails; against principalities and powers, against proximate capital punishment, against all odds.

At the same time: a caution. The story offers no inviolate pattern. The church is at prayer, but no miraculous or infallibly favorable outcome can be adduced. Indeed, we are to remember that angels notwithstanding, Peter, along with this friends, will suffer capital death in due time. Only once, and for a time, was this outcome interfered with. Peter has won a precarious stay of execution only.

We knew all along that in the Syracuse proceedings, the odds against even minimal justice were overwhelming — and prevailed.

Yet we were by no means hopeless, only perhaps chastened, and wary of magic. For we trusted that our friends would hold fast to their resolve; and we were not deceived. We believe that the God of life is with them, and that they will stand firm in that faith. Their ordeal is only the first stage of a vast, seismic shift in public understanding; in it, all the living must have part, eventually. Meantime, such first steps as our friends have dared cannot but be costly. God does not absolve them of the cost, but helps them pay up, in a good spirit, to the farthing.

And beyond all doubt, the church is called, continues to be called, to unremitting prayer. To stand with the prisoners, to attend to their conscience. Standing as our imprisoned friends do, with the voiceless humans, so brutally disregarded, shrugged off, imprisoned, cast aside, perishing of starvation, tortured, capitally disposed of. Utterly powerless, in need (like ourselves) of the delivering ANGEL.

207 The Signs of Peace 207

> Christ has been raised from the dead, the first fruits of those
> who have fallen asleep. (1 Cor. 15, 20)

In a sense that makes sense to me, my friends are already
delivered. They are delivered from fear and trembling
before the power of the state; also from inertia and moral
amnesia. They are fit subjects for the miracle we call
resurrection.

There are others signs in America, in desperate contrast
to the signs my friends are offering. I reflect on one of
these, a monstrous sign, violent, overreaching, a shadow
upon all our lives, upon all of life.

The pentagon. A sign of the dispersal of talent, the
waste of the earth's goods, a monstrous distraction of
mind — from truth and goodness and good sense itself. A
sign, public, bold, shameless, that death is our main intent
and product and obsession. Then this sign in a sense,
breaks up into its components, the large sign into many
smaller ones. Each of which says in minuscule what the
great sign declares in bold face. One walks into the con-
course, the public space beneath the pentagon. Signs
abound. One invites the visitors to undertake a guided
tour of the place. There are opportunities to 'sign up' for
certain courses, offered at the War College nearby. A
veritable neon forest of signs intrudes, offering every
benefit imaginable; such a scene as might greet Hansel and
Gretel in hell. Banking, real estate ('buy now, pay later,'
as they say in the anteroom of hell), a florist, a sandwich
shop, a gift, a car, a piece of jewelry, a bonbon. The
pentagon is in fact, the Complete American Environment.
You make bombs upstairs, you come downstairs to recy-
cle your bomb money; everything your heart (or your
sweetheart's heart) could desire. And everything, just like
hell, under one roof.

I almost forgot. There is a sign leading to a meditation room, at the center of the labyrinth. Another sign announces religious services. (Hell, Dante says, is both time and place. Is there a meditation room in hell? Are religious services held there?)

This strikes me. The signs of peace and peace making, the signs offered by my friends in prison, these lead somewhere. But the multiple signs in the pentagon, the sign of the pentagon itself — these lead exactly nowhere.

In time and place, the pentagon leads nowhere. This I think, is why it is so stark an image of hell — or of a certain culture. America, posting signs that lead to such a place, having led us there, can lead us no further. The signs of the culture, signs of consumerism, racism, sexism, violence — these lead, by one road or another, to the pentagon; inevitably.

And can lead no further. Once in the pentagon, once such a horror is taken for granted, when one has worked there, bought and sold there, made something referred to as a 'living' there — no exit. Hell is being stuck. In just such a place.

The above suggests a contrast. In the gospel of John, we have constant reference to 'signs.' There are certain occurrences, interfering with the normal course of life. These are the very opposite of a dead end. They are meant to lead somewhere. In an obvious sense, the 'signs' lead from illness to health, from sin to innocence restored, from death to life. But something even deeper underlies the matter. The signs offered by Jesus are symbols of healing of spirit. They offer a way out of despair, out of the hopeless numbing that halts the will in its tracks...

To put things mildly, few people any longer are inclined to look for miracles; for signs leading some-

SCOTT FORESMAN PRESS (cont.)

TITLE	GRADE (cont.)	AUTHOR
The New Open Highways Program (cont.)		
Discovering Treasure	5	
Skillbook	5	
Exploring Afar	6	
Skillbook	6	
America, America	7-8	Buggey, Danzer et al
Signal Series		Niles et al

where. Yet according to the gospel, despair cannot claim the final word. We are offered something else; signs of a breakthrough.

It may be that the 'sign' is not offered until we have reached the depths, lost all hope of things worldly, powerful, efficient. Perhaps we must let go, in a sense most unAmerican, of all signs and signals that tell us in so many ways — that we are in charge, that the world yields its mystery and grandeur and riches to our open sesame, that we can indulge in evil means and still bring good ends to pass. All the while of course, we deny spiritual realities and traditions and modes of conduct; deny the possibilities offered by nonviolence and compassion and the call to do justice; deny to ourselves the fruits of prayer, uncommon sense, ecstasy even. We open arms and hearts to the foul signs of the culture, welcome them, buy them, pay for them, place security and hope in them. Even in nuclear arms; which is to say, we scuttle the biblical security of faith in Jesus Christ, taking to heart and soul, the atrocious symbol of omnideath, agreeing in effect, that the Bomb is our savior, along with its makers and hucksters and political slaves and satraps, and the madly bright who squander their talent at the forge of Mars. We declare with all these; we are the miracle makers, believe in us! The Bomb is our security, our Savior, our Sign!

I open the gospel. Do I believe in miracles, in miracles of social and personal healing, in exorcisms of the self damned, in the multiplying of bread, in the liberation of prisoners, including our prisoners of conscience?

There is a greater miracle than any of these. We are told that the crowning 'sign' of Jesus was his own rising from the dead.

Now I take it that this sign, like all others, must lead

somewhere. Must lead, by ways tortuous and long and uphill, though prayer and purified understanding, straight to our own time and place. Here, now, 'sign' of the dead man who walked away from death, when the worst had been done, when the tomb was sealed and the case closed — this sign has become a countersign.

It is for us, here and now, a countersign. It is a sign that goes directly, stupendously counter to the times (the clock of doom, the countdown first strike ethos; time as inevitability of doom); counter also to the places where death stakes its claim (the pentagon, the nuclear white train, the Trident fleet, the bunkers and bases and laboratories where the props and furnishings of hell are deployed).

Our time and place; and people walking mesmerized toward death. And in the same time and place, something else occurring. Some people (not yet all, nor even a large majority) walk in another direction — away from the nuclear mortuary. In the blazing light of Jesus the Countersign, the people go counter. They refuse the doom assigned to them and their children. They renounce hell, that final impasse, and the signs that lead to hell.

The great sign, the sign par excellence, the sign that breaks up, like whiteness into all hues, into all lesser signs — is the rising of Jesus from the dead. And the great sign I hope for (and work on behalf of, and go to jail in view of) is that I and all the living might rise from nuclear death.

The pentagon, that sign of a dead end, that non sign of non life, remains, polluting the atmosphere, a vast hecatomb consecrated to the end of the human adventure. The resurrected Christ, were he to appear there, for healing, or conversion (many of us believe he does appear there) would promptly be arrested. Conversion, we are told, comes hard in hell. Still, I reflect that the sign of resurrection was first raised, not in the heart of Pilate or Herod or the Sanhedrin. It was spelled out first, this sign of hope and rebirth, in the heart of Christ, his beat of love; restored, restoring.

But neither did resurrection stop there. The beat is taken up; it becomes the rhythm of the universe. Our Pilates and Herods and Sanhedrins are not immune from the holy contagion of love. Nor, all thanks to Christ, are we.

The Contributors

Gregory Baum is Professor of Theology and Religious Studies at St. Michael's College in the University of Toronto. He is a member of the editorial committee of the international theological review *Concilium*. His recent publications include *Religion and Alienation* and *The Priority of Labor*.

Daniel Berrigan, S.J., a well-known supporter of peace and human rights, has written many books including *The Discipline of the Mountain*; *A Prison Diary*; and *We Die before We Live: Talking with the Very Ill*.

Robert McAfee Brown is Professor of Theology and Ethics at the Pacific School of Religion. He has written numerous books, including *The Bible Speaks to You*; *Theology in a New Key*; *Gustavo Gutierrez*; *Creative Dislocation — The*

Movement of Grace and his articles have appeared in such publications as *The Christian Century* and *Christianity and Crisis*.

Sidney Callahan, Ph.D., is the author of many books and articles and professor of psychology at Mercy College in New York. She has been married for 31 years and is the mother of six grown children. She has long been active in Catholic lay movements. Her latest book is *Abortion: Understanding Differences*, co-authored with Daniel Callahan.

John Deedy worked in daily journalism in Boston and Worcester, before entering religious journalism in 1951. He edited the diocesan papers of Worcester (1951-59) and Pittsburgh (1959-1967), before moving to *Commonweal* as managing editor, a post he held from 1967-1978. Since then he has free-lanced as a writer of books and correspondent for various publications, including *The Tablet* of London. He is the author of 12 books, most recently *Your Aging Parents*.

John Eagleson is Editor-in-Chief of Orbis Books, and is deeply involved with third world affairs. He spent four years working among the poor in South America; has translated Latin American literature; and is the editor of *Christians & Socialism*, and co-editor, with Philip Scharper, of *The Patriarch's Bible* and *Puebla and Beyond*.

Monika K. Hellwig is Professor of Theology at Georgetown University and President of the Catholic Theological Association. Among her many publications are *The Eucharist and the Hunger of the World; Understanding Catholi-*

cism; *Sign of Reconciliation and Conversion: The Sacrament of Penance for Our Times*, volume 4 of the *Message of the Sacraments* series, of which she is the editor; and *Jesus, The Compassion of God: New Perspectives on the Tradition of Christianity*.

Theodore M. Hesburgh, C.S.C., an internationally respected educator and author, is President of the University of Notre Dame.

Kathleen Hughes, R.S.C.J., is Assistant Professor of Liturgy at Catholic Theological Union in Chicago and serves on various commissions such as the International Commission on English in the Liturgy and the Advisory Board of the Bishops' Committee on the Liturgy. She is a member of the editorial committee for the liturgy volumes of *Concilium* and has published widely on liturgical subjects.

Father Robert P. Imbelli received his Ph.D. in philosophical theology from Yale University. Since 1978 he has been Professor of Systematic Theology in the Maryknoll School of Theology. He has also been visiting lecturer at Princeton Theological Seminary and Fordham University. His articles and reviews have appeared in *Commonweal*, *Theology Today*, *Review for Religious*, and *America*.

Marie Augusta Neal, S.N.D. de Namur, who received a Ph.D. from Harvard University in sociology, is Professor of Sociology at Emmanuel College in Boston. Among her many publications are *Values and Interests in Social Change*; *A Sociotheology of Letting Go*; and *Catholic Sisters in Transition from the 1960s to the 1980s*.

M. Basil Pennington, O.C.S.O. is a Cistercian (Trappist) monk of the Abbey of Our Lady of St. Joseph in Spencer Massachusetts. With Thomas Merton he started Cistercian Publications in 1968 and founded the Institute of Cistercian Studies at Western Michigan University in 1973. Father has published over dozen books, including *O Holy Mountain: Journal of a Retreat on Mount Athos*; and *Challenges in Prayer,* volume 1 of the *Ways of Prayer* series, for which he is consulting Editor.

Donald Senior, C.P. is Professor of New Testament Studies at the Catholic Theological Union in Chicago. He is the author of several books and numerous articles on biblical subjects including the 4-volume *Passion Series.* He is co-editor of the *New Testament Message* series.

Carroll Stuhlmueller, C.P. is Professor of Old Testament Studies at Catholic Theological Union in Chicago and editor of *The Bible Today.* He is past President of the Catholic Biblical Association and of the Chicago Society of Biblical Research. He has authored numerous books and articles and recently completed a 2-volume commentary on the Psalms for the *Old Testament Message* series, for which he is co-editor.